100% BIZARRE, OBSCURE, RANDOM

THE BOOK OF PERCENTAGES

AND SURPRISINGLY ENLIGHTENING FACTS ON JUST ABOUT EVERYTHING ~~EVERYTHING~~
∧
NOTHING

TOM PHILBIN

Aadamsmedia

Avon, Massachusetts

Published by
Adams Media, a division of F+W Media, Inc.
57 Littlefield Street, Avon, MA 02322. U.S.A.
www.adamsmedia.com

ISBN 10: 1-60550-108-5
ISBN 13: 978-1-60550-108-6

Printed in the United States of America.

J I H G F E D C B A

Library of Congress Cataloging-in-Publication Data
is available from the publisher.

This book is available at quantity discounts for bulk purchases.
For information, please call 1-800-289-0963.

Thanks to my brother Mike, who did extensive research on the book
and wrote a number of the entries.

Introduction

A funny thing happened to me as I wrote this book. Normally when I write something, I read it over for sense and accuracy after I'm finished. But this book was different. As I read over the various entries, I found myself engrossed in many of them, as though I were reading them for the first time. I surely hope you have a similar reaction.

The entries cover a wide variety of topics from animals to transportation, diet to medical matters, celebrities to pets, gender relations to the home—and many more present a wide variety of facts where the frequency or degree—or the infrequency of—are described in terms of percentages, which are often interesting and surprising in and of themselves. Each entry was selected by me and had a simple criteria: is it interesting? The book is not meant to be an encyclopedic reference on reality but, rather, an entertaining read where one can get a quick grasp of the facts and an overview of a subject. For example: **90%** of all dog owners give their dogs gifts at Christmas and on their birthdays; **30%** of all dog owners carry a picture of their dog in their wallets; and **25%** percent of owners surveyed said they have missed work because of their dog's illnesses. Collectively what does this entry tell us? That most dog owners love their dogs to a degree perhaps not yet realized by readers who don't own dogs.

There are many other entries that are similarly entertaining as well as enlightening, such as ones where the sex practices of teenagers give us a tremendous insight into what their lives are like. You also get a sense of how dangerous it is to be young in the wild and how only the strong survive when you read the percentages. In some entries, too, I have been constrained to give people what amounts to advice. For example, there are some entries focusing on rip-offs on such things as wet basements and mold remediation, and I tell you how to handle such problems without paying someone a chunk of your hard-earned cash! Some entries are light and entertaining—such as the one that recounts how many cats snore—some are not. However, you can be guaranteed that no matter the topic, you'll learn a lot.

Perhaps you will choose your own favorite entries, such as the one where the question posed is how many people have an alcoholic drink for breakfast. Surprisingly, if you make under $20,000 a year you might be among the **20%** in that group who have a drink, and if you make over $100,000 a year you might be among the **33%** who imbibes with breakfast. I can hear it now:

"What will you have for breakfast, honey?"

"Two eggs up, hash brown, rye toast, and a boilermaker."

Some entries are short. Some are long. But in all cases I was mindful that this book is not just a presentation of data—of percentages—but that I should try to put the numbers in the context of why a certain percentage is what it is. For example, the fastest animal in the United States is the pronghorn antelope, which is **35%** faster than a race horse, and can run sixty-five miles per hour for the better part of an hour. *Why*, you ask? To find out, you'll have to read on. . . . Indeed, with all the information that this book presents, it may as well be called *The Book of Percentages—Plus*!

I hope you get **100%** enjoyment out of this book. I know I did.

Tom Philbin

What percentage of movies are given an R-rating?

More than half of all films—**55%**—have been R-rated. **24%** have been rated PG. **10%** have been rated **PG-13**, since this rating came into existence in 1984. Only **8%** of all films have received a G-rating and **3%** rated NC-17, which replaced the X-rating in 1990.

WHAT PERCENTAGE OF PROSPECTIVE EMPLOYERS ARE CHECKING JOB CANDIDATES OUT ON THE INTERNET?

You may be surprised at the number of companies who really are checking out their employees—prospective or otherwise—online. **61%** of companies are doing online background checks and, in **43%** of these cases, job candidates were not hired because of the negative information these companies found. When they looked online, hiring managers discovered that **31%** of prospects had lied about their qualifications, **24%** were linked to criminal behavior, **19%** had bad-mouthed their former or present company, **19%** boasted about doing drugs or drinking, **15%** spread confidential information from former employers, **11%** posted suggestive photographs, and **8%** had a screen name that created a poor first impression. Since the advent of Facebook, MySpace, and even Google, people don't realize that much of the information they post is public information, but you need to be careful. Always think twice before posting info that can hurt your chances of getting—or keeping—a job.

> Sex appeal is **50%** what you've got and **50%** what people think you've got.
>
> Sophia Loren, Italian actress

What kinds of movies are watched by the highest percentage of people?

This depends, of course, on who you ask. The percentage of people watching movies with positive moral content has increased by **163%** over the last several years. Viewership of movies that provide an uplifting, redemptive experience has also increased by **337%**.

How many doctors don't follow appropriate hand-washing guidelines?

The disgusting truth is that more than half—**60%**—of all doctors don't wash their hands when they are supposed to. Take control of your health and ask your doctors to wash their hands if you don't observe them doing so.

Talent counts **30%**, appearance counts **70%**.

Chinese proverb

IF YOUR CHILD WERE GUILTY OF A NONVIOLENT CRIME, WOULD YOU TELL THE COPS?

Talk about a parent's love! Only **32%** of parents said they would sing like a canary; **68%** would keep their mouths shut.

Are Americans honest?

Americans aren't doing too badly in the honesty category with **48%** considering themselves to be very honest, **50%** believing themselves to be somewhat honest, and only **2%** admitting to not being very honest at all.

What percentage of young men have been forcibly removed from a wedding?

We've all seen those wedding videos where a drunken groomsman tries to beat up the groom/ swing from a chandelier/make out with an unwilling bridesmaid. Turns out that **5%** of young men have been removed from weddings for this type of bad behavior.

What percentage of people are left-handed?

Between **7%** and **10%** of the population is left-handed. There are a variety of causes for this inclination, including exposure to higher-than-normal rates of testosterone, genetic facts, and the effect of ultrasound on the brain. Left-handedness appears more frequently in males than females, in identical twins, and in a variety of groups of people afflicted with neurological disorders such as Down syndrome and mental retardation. For years, being a southpaw carried a social stigma, but this has largely faded, though some people still feel oppressed. The list of the many famous left-handed people includes Bill Clinton, Harry Truman, Supreme Court Justice Ruth Bader Ginsburg, military figures such as Julius Caesar and Alexander the Great, automaker Henry Ford, Benjamin Franklin, Helen Keller, and entertainers Jay Leno and David Letterman.

Which gender more commonly stalks the other?

Men stalk more frequently than women. **75%** of stalkers are men, leaving women to make up that extra **25%**. All told, experts estimate that there are 1.4 million stalkers in America. There are a number of things to be aware of, some of them quite upsetting, but don't worry too much. The first stalking law was instituted in 1990 in California; now all fifty states have them.

How many people aged eighteen and older have never been married?

60% of Americans have never been married. Another **25%** are divorced, and **15%** are widowed.

What percentage of American households own a horse?

4% of all Americans own at least one horse and **3%** board their horse at home. It appears that, if you're a horse owner, you also own a dog. **80%** of all of horse owners seem to prescribe to this logic.

❝ 80% of success is showing up. ❞

Woody Allen, U.S. actor

5

> "Harpists spend **90%** of their lives tuning their harps and **10%** playing out of tune."
>
> Igor Stravinsky, Russian-born composer

What is America's favorite spectator sport?

Astonishingly, football blew away the competition with **43%** of the population judging it as their favorite sport. Baseball came in second with a popularity rating of only **12%**—surprising, considering that baseball is "America's past time." Following baseball was basketball at **11%,** hockey at **4%,** and auto racing at **3%**. Ice skating and golf came in as the least popular sports with an approval rating of **2%** and **2%** respectively.

HOW LONG SHOULD A MAN HAVE DATED A WOMAN BEFORE PASSING GAS IN FRONT OF HER?

While **34%** of women believe that this should never be deemed acceptable, many women disagreed. **39%** of women believe that a man should wait until they have officially become boyfriend and girlfriend. **13%** think a man should at least wait until the end of a first date, and **12%** of women wanted that moment to wait until they were living together. The remaining **2%** believed the question was too gross to answer.

What percentage of the time do celebrity marriages end in divorce?

Perhaps this comes as no surprise, but celebrity marriages break up an average of **50%** of the time, compared to **31%** for non-celebs. Among the main reasons for this high divorce rate is the constant temptation of beautiful men and women coming out of the proverbial woodwork and the weak personalities of actors and actresses who could not avoid the temptation.

How much confidence do Americans have in the government's ability to protect its citizens from terrorist attacks?

Only **16%** of Americans have a great deal of confidence in the government's ability to protect them against attack. The greatest number of people—**57%**—have a fair amount of trust, **23%** admit to having limited confidence, and **4%** have almost no confidence in the government's abilities at all!

WHAT DO VOTERS CONSIDER THE MOST IMPORTANT CHARACTER TRAITS IN PRESIDENTIAL CANDIDATES?

47% of the people consider honesty to be the most important trait a candidate can have, followed by a "take-charge" personality, which is important to **21%** of the voting public. A down-to-earth ability to connect with ordinary people is important to **21%** as well, with an even-tempered personality being important to only **7%**. Last, but not least, **4%** of voters want a candidate to have a strong religious faith.

HOW FAST IS FAST FOOD?

Very fast. Roughly **68%** of people in fast food drive-through lines will not wait more than five minutes. So, in order to hang onto their customers, more and more fast-food joints are allowing their clientele to order food electronically, so it's ready when they arrive. Pizza chains are in the lead on this. For example, Pizza Hut gets thirty electronic orders a minute, and the company's online ordering has increased by **600%** in the last three years. Pizza Hut is not alone. Chipotle first offered online ordering in 2006 and that has increased by over **40%**. Next on the menu appears to be text messaged orders.

How many American homes have two TVs?

80% of all American homes have two TVs and **50%** have three.

WHAT PERCENT OF PEOPLE WASH PRODUCE BEFORE CONSUMPTION?

Only **71%** of vegetable eaters wash their fruits and vegetables before sitting down to eat. This means **29%** do not, which is a risky idea considering the bacteria that can lurk in leafy greens and unwashed fruits and vegetables.

WHAT PERCENTAGE OF AMERICANS HAVE DISCUSSED THE TOPIC OF RACISM WITH A PERSON OF A DIFFERENT RACE?

A large majority! **83%** of males have broached the topic, along with **64%** of females, **72%** of whites, **70%** of blacks, and **84%** of those who identify as "other."

WHAT IS THE LIFE OF A MUSICIAN LIKE?

While they're on their way to becoming professional musicians, the majority of musicians—like actors or actresses—must hold other jobs in order to survive. **40%** are self-employed. The rest work regularly for someone else. The majority of those who follow this path earn between $10.81 and $36.55 an hour. However, **10%** of all musicians basically earn minimum wage. Musicians in the top **10%** of moneymakers do quite well, earning roughly $57.37 an hour. Of course, the superstars of music can earn just about anything.

❝ You can learn a lot from the client. . . . Some **70%** doesn't matter, but **30%** will kill you. **❞**

Paul J. Paulson, U.S. business executive

What percentage of Americans play fantasy sports?

With the popularity of fantasy sports continuing to grow, **5%** of adults now participate in a fantasy league. Men are more likely to participate than women and younger men are more likely to play than those who are older.

What are the odds that a burglary in the United States will be solved?

You would think that figuring out who robbed your home and stole your forty-two-inch plasma TV would be a high priority for police departments around the country. That may or may not be true, but only around **14%** of all home burglars are brought to justice.

What percentage of animals has been driven to extinction?

As a result of mismanagement, pollution, and the territorial encroachment of the growing human population, **33%** of animals have been lost forever. The implications of this tragedy on humanity cannot be fully envisioned at this point, but surely it is not good.

Have teen pregnancies increased?

Unfortunately, teen pregnancy is on the rise. In recent years, the amount of pregnancies has increased by **15%**.

WHAT PERCENTAGE OF AMERICANS BELIEVE IN CREATIONISM?

Close to **64%** of people want creationism, which is generally understood as the creation story based on the Book of Genesis, to be taught hand in hand with evolution in public schools. Only **48%** of these people accept any form of evolution, even if guided by God, and a mere **26%** accept Darwin's theory of evolution. **42%** of those polled believe that all living things—plant, animal, and human—have existed in their present form since the beginning of time.

Also, **27%** of college students believe that creatures have always existed in their present form, and they are joined by **50%** of high school graduates, and **42%** of people who attended, but didn't graduate from college.

Are American kids too cool for school?

Nationally, about **75%** of children ages twelve to seventeen are doing fine academically, performing at or above the grade level they are in. Additionally, **25%** of the children in this age bracket are in a gifted class. Girls do better than boys, and children with married parents do better than those with parents who are divorced, widowed, or never married.

What Protestant religious group is most common?

For decades, the most common denomination was mainstream liberal Protestantism, but now Fundamentalist denominations have taken over. In 2003, only **46%** of American Protestants identified themselves with mainline Protestant denominations as compared to **59%** in 1960.

What percentage of men have dated someone ten years older than they are?

Cougar alert! **24%** of men have dated someone at least ten years older than they are.

How would you like to be told if a man isn't into you?

Even though it hurts, **38%** of women would like the guy to be honest and straightforward. They don't want to be strung along. **34%** want the guy to wait a few days, then call and let them down gently. **26%** of women just want the guy to spare their feelings by taking their number and then simply never calling.

How many American women are prostitutes?

Astonishing—and sad—**1%**, or one million American women, prostitute themselves. **80%** of these women cite drug use as the reason behind their illicit activity. You can't buy drugs if you don't have any money and, oftentimes, prostitutes are heavily addicted.

Do eggs help on a diet?

The answer is yes! The amount of calories found in two eggs is better than the equivalent number of calories in a bagel because they keep people feeling fuller until the next meal. Indeed, people who start their day with eggs as part of a low calories diet lose **65%** more weight than their peers who begin their day with bagels.

How experienced are today's air traffic controllers?

Today's air traffic controllers are **25%** trainees, a number that has gone up **100%** in the last year. Meanwhile, the experienced controllers (**75%**) have increased their workload by up to **50%**. Have a nice flight!

What percentage of couples call off their weddings per year?

The question is: if you're not sure you want to get married, why propose or accept the ring? Well, **20%** of couples each year—almost 500,000 people—will call off their nuptials.

> **80%** were hypocrites, **80%** liars, **80%** serious sinners . . . except on Sundays. There is always boozing and floozying . . . I don't have enough time to tell you everybody's name.

William "Fishbait" Miller, Congressional doorkeeper

How strong is a male Orangutan?

Male orangutans, who live mainly in Sumatra and Borneo, tip the scales at 90kg (200lb). The orangutan is the largest tree-dweller, and is roughly **400%** stronger than a man. But, despite this difference, orangutans often seem closer to humans than other creatures in terms of their abilities. For example, these giants have been seen creating primitive tools, which they use to probe into narrow crevasses to gain leverage as well as to find food.

Has the number of multiple births increased?

Very much so! With the advent of fertility treatments, we are seeing more and more multiple births in the news. In fact, the rate of multiple births has increased by **65%** between 1980 and the present.

What percentage of the time does an exterior of a building require heavy preparation, such as scraping or priming, before the surface can be renewed?

If the surface is painted, it will only need this prepartion **10%** of the time. If the surface has a penetrating stain on it then chances are that less than **5%** that prep of any kind will be needed, because penetrating stain—the kind that seeps down into the wood—doesn't peel.

"I'll take **50%** efficiency to get to one **100%** loyalty."

Samuel Goldwyn, U.S. film producer

WHAT PERCENTAGE OF YOUNG AMERICANS CAN ANSWER THE QUESTION: WHERE IN THE WORLD IS CARMEN SAN DIEGO?

Apparently geography is not young America's strong suit! **50%** of Americans between the ages of eighteen and twenty-four don't know the locations of countries where important news is being made. **66%** don't know where Iraq is; only **23%** of college kids know where Saudi Arabia, Iran, Iraq, and Israel are located; and an almost unbelievable **94%** of high school graduates also have no idea.

WHAT HELPED INCREASE THE AMERICAN LITERACY RATE IN THE LATE 1800s?

In 1880 there were only 800 public schools in the entire United States, but by 1900 that number of schools had vaulted to 11,000. As a consequence, the literacy rate increased from **11%** to **17%**. This achievement is all the more remarkable because, during this time period, most of the immigrants arriving on America's shores did not speak a word of English. These immigrants had a burning desire to learn, and for many it was the first time they were in a society where there were no laws against learning.

"99% of requested deaths go unrecorded. It's a secret crime."

Derek Humphry, Director of the Hemlock Society

WHAT AREAS IN THE UNITED STATES ARE PRONE TO EARTHQUAKES?

As we all know, California is the state most prone to serious earthquakes. In fact, there is a **99.7%** chance that California will experience another substantial quake over the next thirty years. However, California isn't the only state looking forward to rockin' and rollin'. A seismic zone in central United States which runs through Arkansas, Missouri, Tennessee, and Kentucky has a **97%** chance of quaking before 2035. New England, though not as prone to earthquakes as other parts of the country, still has a **0.064%** chance of experiencing a seriously earth-shaking quake.

WHAT PERCENTAGE OF WOMEN COLOR THEIR HAIR?

Women are certainly determined to banish their grays! A full **75%** of women color their hair to either hide grays, get natural looking highlights, or just play around with their hair color. Maybe some want to answer that eternal question: Do blondes really have more fun?

What is the unemployment rate in Iraq?

Since 2003, between **27%** to **60%** of all Iraqi citizens have been unemployed.

Koala bears, found only in Australia, belong to a class of animals that are among the oldest inhabitants of the planet. They have one of the most specialized diets of any living mammal, feeding exclusively on eucalyptus leaves. Koalas have a lifespan of around eighteen years and are certainly rated among the world's most tired animals, sleeping away **75%** of their day—eighteen hours—every day.

What percentage of Americans know their sun sign?

Most Americans have no idea what it means for the moon to be in the seventh house, but, with horoscopes in a large majority of magazines and newspapers, close to **90%** know their sun sign.

"**90%** of the politicians give the other **10%** a bad reputation."

Henry Kissinger, German-born American political scientist, diplomat, and Nobel Peace Prize winner

What percentage of men don't brush their teeth every day?

We all know that the dentist recommends that everyone brush their teeth at least twice a day, but only **40%** of men follow this recommendation.

Have sales of bottled water recently increased or decreased?

Despite a variety of campaigns organized to encourage Americans to drink tap, the amount of bottled water we drink has actually increased. Right now, we are drinking **10%** more bottled water than we did the year before.

What percentage of readers prefer to read a print copy of a book?

Despite the fact that we live in an electronic age and there are multiple e-book readers available, **82%** still say that they prefer curling up with a printed book over reading online, or using an electronic reading device.

Do Americans like superstores?

You bet we do! Americans love superstores, and at a cost to tradition-al retailers. Due to the fact that we virtually invade warehouse-style stores like Wal-Mart, Costco, and Target and like to capitalize on the convenience and savings, the sales of traditional retailers plummeted to **69%**.

What percent of the world's oceans are polluted due to humans?

Humans have a huge impact on the environment! In fact, **80%** of all marine debris—such as trash and toxic matter—originally comes from shore-based activities such as picnics and beach outings.

IS IT A GOOD IDEA TO WEAR SUNGLASSES?

Everyone should absolutely wear sunglasses whenever possible since ultraviolet rays can permanently damage your eyes. It's impossible to tell whether a pair of sunglasses offers adequate protection by looking at the darkness of the lenses or whether the lenses have a mirrored effect. To give protection, lenses must have a UV coating, which is colorless. There are three categories of sunglasses. Cosmetic glasses block at least **70%** of UVB rays and **20%** of UVA rays. General purpose glasses block at least **95%** of UVB rays and **60%** of UVA rays. And Special purpose glasses must block at least **99%** of UVB rays and **60%** of UVA rays.

WHAT DRIVES WOMEN TO COMMIT MURDER?

Every crime has a motive—and murders committed by women are no exception. Of the following percentages, women often admitted to having more than one motive, making the percentages add up to more than **100%**. **74%** of women murder for money or financial gain; **13%** murder to seize control of a situation. **11%** commit murder because they find the act enjoyable. **10%** of women are motivated by sex and **24%** murder due to involvement in drugs or a cult, to cover up another crime, or because they wish to diminish feelings of inadequacy.

I believe **100%** in the power and importance of music.

James Taylor, U.S. musician

WHO ARE THE TOP FIVE PRO BASKETBALL COACHES OF ALL TIME?

5. Larry Brown was known as getting the best out of mediocre teams. He coached for twenty-five years and had a winning record of **57%**. He was also the only coach to ever lead both an NBA and college team to a championship, coaching the Kansas Jayhawks to the title in 1988 and the Detroit Pistons to the championship in 2004.

4. Pat Riley, who coached the star studded L.A. Lakers in the 1980s, compiled a 1210–694 record—that's a **63%** winning record! He stacked up five championships and won 171 playoff games.

3. Gregg Popovich is the coach of the San Antonio Spurs and had a **.646%** winning record and eleven consecutive winning seasons.

2. Red Auerbach, the coach of the Boston Celtics had a **.662%** winning record or a 823–426 record.

1. Phil Jackson is arguably the best coach of all time with nine championships, a 980–418 record, and **.703%** winning record. He also has the most playoff wins at 193.

WHAT FEMALE CELEBRITY TATTOOS ARE DISLIKED THE MOST?

23% of Americans dislike Pamela Anderson's tattoo of twisted thorns and **18%** of Americans disliked Angelina Jolie's "Billy Bob" tattoo, which has since been lasered off. Americans also dislike Pink's necklace tattoo that features a tattooed crucifix. These ugly celebrity tats should serve as a warning to all of us to look before we leap—it's much more difficult to remove a tattoo than it is to ink it on.

WHAT PERCENTAGE OF OUR BEE POPULATION HAS DISAPPEARED?

Bees are very important as they pollinate some **30%** of the country's food supply. Unfortunately, over the past few years, these important bees have been dying in droves. To date, we have lost some **50%** of our bee population, though the loss has not impacted food supply yet.

What is killing them? Various things are suspected, including pollution, a virus, pesticides, and parasites that weaken the bees' immune systems. Once a hive has been compromised, death can come fast. A hive of 12,000 bees can fall to less than 100 in three weeks or less—an event described as "colony collapse disorder." Something has to be done and quickly, because experts say that one in every three bites of food depends upon the pollination of bees.

> "We don't know a millionth of **1%** about anything."
>
> Thomas Edison, U.S. inventor

What percentage of Americans follow professional football?

We are a nation of football lovers! **65%** of men are ready for some football, compared to **39%** of women.

HOW DOES DIET AFFECT FERTILITY?

It's not surprising to find out that what you eat affects how you procreate. Some foods help a woman become more fertile; others decrease her ability to become pregnant. Some of the culprits may be shocking! Carbohydrates that are digested quickly like white rice and potatoes are likely to decrease fertility by **92%**! Animal proteins decrease fertility by **39%**. Don't worry, though, you can combat the negative effects of these popular foods by taking a daily multivitamin. This will reduce the chance of infertility by up to **40%**!

HOW FAST IS THE PRONGHORN ANTELOPE?

While the fastest race horse (a "quarter horse") can run up to forty-five miles an hour, the pronghorn antelope—found chiefly in Wyoming—is capable of running up to sixty-five miles an hour. That's **35%** faster! The astonishing thing about the antelope (which happens to be the fastest creature in the United States) is that it can keep up its speed for an hour! How? For one thing, its heart is twice the size that it needs to be to successfully operate its cardiovascular system! It also has a tremendous ability to turn oxygen into energy, and a lean, muscular body like a deer.

What percentage of Americans support the death penalty?

An overwhelming majority of people—**69%**—support the use of the death penalty. **27%** are against it and **4%** have no opinion. People are also not shy about advocating its use. Only **21%** felt the death penalty was used too often.

What states have the highest percentage of residents who were not born in America?

There are certain states that have high numbers of immigrant populations. This is mainly due to their locations and historical importance. **27.4%** of California residents have been born elsewhere. **21.8%** of New Yorkers come from other countries, as do **18.9%** of Floridians.

How many arson fires are set yearly and who sets them?

Every year in the United States 500,000 fires are set. These fires kill more than 700 Americans a year and are the second leading cause of residential fire deaths.

Who sets these fires? You'd be surprised! Close to **75%** of firefighters in this country are volunteers and, in an ironic twist, hundreds of convicted arsonists have come from their ranks.

What percentage of people believe in a literal interpretation of the Bible?

33.33% of those polled believe in a literal interpretation of the Bible, while **60%** believe that the predictions in the Book of Revelations will come true.

Where do Americans buy their books?

The top three retail choices for buying books are buying on-line **(77%)**, buying books from a chain bookstore **(76%)**, and buying from an independent bookstore **(49%)**.

What percentage of Americans believe capital punishment is an appropriate penalty for murder?

The race here is almost dead even. **47%** believe the death penalty is the most appropriate punishment for murder. **48%** believe life imprisonment without the possibility of parole is more appropriate, and **5%** have no opinion on the matter.

WHAT PERCENTAGE OF NASA SPACE MISSIONS LAUNCH ON TIME?

40% of NASA space missions launch on time. Airlines beat this hands down, with a **73%** on-time record, but space travel involves a much more complicated piece of machinery. The space shuttles took off on time in 47 of their 118 missions. Half the delays were caused by technical problems and additionally, there are weather delays, including hurricanes, and tropical storms. There is also an instance of a delay occurring due to a woodpecker hammering away on the space shuttle's fuel tank.

What percentage of men take their laptops on vacation?

Unfortunately, you can take your job with you on vacation—and **15%** of men are choosing to do just that. After all, nothing says relaxation like an umbrella drink, a tropical beach, and an e-mail from your boss!

90% of everything is crap.

Theodore Sturgeon, American science fiction writer

What percentage of Americans believe the United States is winning the war on terrorism?

Only **29%** of Americans believe the United States is winning against terrorism; **20%** of Americans believe the terrorists are winning the war; **50%** feel that neither side is winning. **44%** of Americans are very or somewhat worried about being victims of terrorism, a percentage that has been stable since late 2005.

How much water do you need to stay healthy?

Rumor has it that you're supposed to drink eight cups of water a day to stay healthy, but recent studies have found that we only need to drink enough to stave off thirst. It's also important to keep in mind that we in-take water in other ways than drinking. Foods that are rich in water, such as lettuce, broccoli, grapefruit, carrots, and soup provide us with about **20%** of our necessary H_2O each day.

Does laughing make you healthier?

There is little doubt that this is the case. Laughing can increase your heart rate by **10%** to **20%** which means you can burn an extra ten to forty calories a day. Over a year that can add up to a four-pound weight loss.

"80% of married men cheat in America. The rest cheat in Europe."

Jackie Mason, American comedian

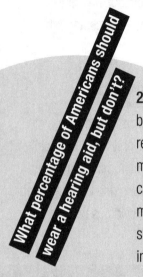

What percentage of Americans should wear a hearing aid, but don't?

20% of Americans should invest in a hearing aid, but refuse. Ego is certainly suspected as a main reason for this phenomenon, particularly since many of these Americans are members of the so-called iPod generation. To combat this reluctance, manufacturers make hearing aids in a variety of shapes including teardrop and triangle, and colors including green and deep red.

How much oil is under the Arctic Circle?

The area north of the Arctic Ocean probably contains **13%** of the world's undiscovered oil—some 90 billion barrels—and **33%** of its undiscovered natural gas.

WHAT ARE THE CHANCES OF HAVING YOUR BOOK MADE INTO A MOVIE?

I'm sorry to tell you this, but your chances are actually quite slim. However, you do have a better shot at getting your book made into a movie than you do winning the lottery. It is estimated by insiders that only **1%** of books are optioned by a movie company, and only one in a thousand actually goes into production and makes it to the silver screen.

Of course, if your movie does make it to the big screen, you can earn a pot of money in one fell swoop. When Lawrence Sanders sold his first novel, *The Anderson Tapes*, to the movies he earned $25,000 from the hardcover publisher, $200,000 from the paperback publisher, and another $250,000 from the movie producer—and he earned all this money within a week!

How much of a cut did Heidi Fleiss get from the beautiful women she prostituted?

Fleiss—the infamous Hollywood Madam—pimped out beautiful, expensive call girls in places like St. Tropez, New York, and Los Angeles. These girls served people with deep pockets and Fleiss's share was **40%** of each assignation. When questioned, Fleiss said that today money, rather than sex, motivates her and she won't even sit down for an interview without being paid.

WHAT MOUNTAIN HAS THE HIGHEST FATALITY RATES?

Annapurna, in central Nepal, is over 26,000 feet high making it the tenth highest worldwide. The peak is famous for spontaneous avalanches, and 53 out of the 130 climbers who attempted ascent have lost their lives, making for a **41%** fatality rate.

How can waitresses receive higher tips?

Waitresses who write "thank you" on checks before giving them to their customers receive **11%** more in tips than those who don't. Waitresses who give information about an upcoming dinner special on the checks receive **17%** to **20%** higher.

How does weight affect the odds of contracting cancer?

Gaining more than eleven pounds after the age of eighteen increases one's odds for contracting all kinds of cancer. Women who gain more than twenty pounds have a **40%** higher risk of contracting cancer than women who gain just five pounds.

What percentage of kids have a TV in their bedroom?

43% of children under the age of two have a TV in their bedroom; **30%** of kids under age three have a TV in their rooms, as do **43%** of children ages four to six.

What percentage of Americans believe breakfast is the most important meal of the day?

90% believe that breakfast is incredibly important, yet only **49%** of us eat it regularly. Breakfast is important because bile and toxins build up in the body overnight and food works to balance out our systems. Breakfast is also important because it fuels our bodies. Just like you can't run a car without gas, your body can't run without breakfast. Hey! Leggo my Eggo!

What is the Earth's atmosphere made up of?

Oxygen makes up **21%** of our atmosphere, nitrogen **78%,** and a mixture of other gases comprise the remaining **1%.** Almost all the oxygen in the Earth's atmophere has been produced by living organisms and the Amazon rainforest produces more than **20%** of the world's oxygen supply.

WHO DOES THE HUNTING IN A PRIDE OF LIONS?

Interestingly—although she normally weighs **20%** less than the male—the lioness hunts for her pride. Lionesses don't have a lot of stamina due to their relatively small hearts; a male's heart makes up to **0.57%** of his body weight, while a female's heart makes up only **0.45%.** Therefore, while females can reach speeds of about forty miles an hour, they have to be close to prey before charging and will run out of gas quickly. However, despite these limitations, lionesses are successful for a number of reasons. First, they attack as a group. Second, a number of females encircle their prey and conceal themselves where their prey can't see them until it's too late. The lioness completes her kill by biting down and cutting off the unfortunate animal's air supply or, if the prey is small enough, with a single swipe of a paw. Lionesses will rarely attack large, healthy animals such as water buffalos or giraffes because of the possibility of injury. Indeed, one kick from a giraffe's powerful hind leg has been known to decapitate a lion or lioness.

> ❝Human beings are **7%** water, and with some the rest is collagen.❞
>
> Martin Mull, American actor

What percentage of a cucumber is made up of water?

A cucumber is **96%** water.

What percentage of the human body is made up of water?

This percentage varies by person, gender, and age. Babies' bodies are made up of roughly **78%** H_2O, but by one year of age, that amount drops to about **65%**. About **60%** of the bodies of adult men are water, compared to **55%** of the bodies of adult women. Fat men also have a lower percentage of water than thin men.

HOW MANY PEOPLE THINK THEY ARE UNDERPAID?

Close to **51%** of workers believe that they are not paid enough for their jobs, compared with **46%** of workers who say they are paid about the right amount, and **3%** said they were overpaid.

Lower-paid workers were more likely to say that they are underpaid. Among those who earn less than $75,000, **62%** of respondents said they are underpaid, compared with **38%** of workers who earn $75,000 or more. Women **(55%)** were more likely than men **(47%)** to say they are underpaid for the work they do.

HOW MANY PARAKEETS TALK TO PEOPLE?

Not many parakeets can tell their owners that they want a cracker. Actually, only **5%** of parakeets make sounds that are recognizable as human speech. The reason for this low percentage is that parakeets talk to demonstrate an extreme connection with their owners, and because it takes them a very long time—months or years—to be able to reproduce human speech. The effort that they put forth to communicate is, in a way, a reflection of how much the bird cares for its owner or owners.

What percentage of people believe that it is dishonest to "regift" a present?

74% of people said they thought it was dishonest, while **26%** said they didn't think so at all. My guess is that those **74%** never received a truly horrible present from their in-laws!

"Don't tell your problems to people: **80%** don't care; and the other **20%** are glad you have them."

Lou Holtz, American author and former NCAA and NFL head coach

What percentage of women think the Internet has been the biggest breakthrough of the century?

75% of women are logging on, blogging, and IMing away!

What percentage of women had obtained a bachelor's degree by the year 2003?

31% of women aged twenty-four to twenty-nine had earned a bachelor's degree or higher by 2003. In comparison, **26%** of men had earned their BA by that time. More women—**88%**—had also graduated from high school than men—**86%**.

Travel is **90%** anticipation and **10%** recollection. Edward Streeter, American novelist

WHAT ARE THE MAIN CAUSES OF FATAL CAR ACCIDENTS CAUSED BY TEENAGERS?

The causes of these accidents vary. Speeding is a factor in **35%** of deaths. Cell phone usage is also dangerous. It increases the likelihood of a crash by **300%**. Having a passenger in the car—which can cause the driver to be distracted—increases the likelihood of a fatal crash by **48%**. A second passenger increases that risk by **158%**. The radio is another distraction—and the likelihood of an accident rises **87%**. Lack of sleep is another disturbing factor. It is estimated that around **50%** of teenagers are sleep-deprived and **55%** of crashes involving teenagers are caused by fatigue. Also, disturbingly, **25%** of teen drivers were found to have been drinking.

WHAT PERCENTAGE DOES A LITERARY AGENT CHARGE FOR SELLING YOUR BOOK?

Years ago agents would take **10%** of everything you were paid by the American publisher for the book. He or she would get extra for selling the book to a foreign publisher or publishers. However, a number of years ago the percentage was changed to **15%** for sales to American publishers and **20%** for sales to foreign publishers. If you're looking to sell a book, watch out! Legitimate agents won't charge you any fees. When the publisher pays the agent, he takes out his percentage and sends the rest on to you!

In most cases, the publisher will give you what is called an advance against royalties. All this means is that the publisher gives you money to finance you while you are writing the book, which you repay when the book is published. A certain percentage is paid to the publisher until you pay back the advance.

What state raises the most turkeys?

With 271 million turkeys—valued at $3.7 million—raised in the United States on a yearly basis, there are a lot of turkeys to go around. Minnesota is the top producer, followed by North Carolina, Arkansas, Virginia, Missouri, and Indiana. These six states together account for about **66%** of all U.S. turkeys.

How many high schools offer driver's education?

Only **20%** of high schools are willing to teach teens to drive, a precipitous drop from the **90%** of schools offering the program in the 1990s. Fingers point at budget cuts as the main culprit for this decline in driver's ed.

What percentage of women aged sixteen and over work in a professional specialty?

34% of women aged sixteen or older work in administrative or managerial jobs compared to only **30%** of men.

HOW COMMON IS DRINKING IN AMERICA?

Excessive alcohol use, which takes on two different forms, is the third leading lifestyle-related cause of death for people in the United States each year. Approximately **5%** of the population drinks heavily. (Heavy drinking is defined as drinking more than two drinks a day on average for men or more than one drink per day on average for women.) Close to **15%** binge drink. (Binge drinking is defined as drinking five or more drinks during a single sitting for men or four or more drinks during a single occasion for women.) Both forms of excessive drinking can lead to a variety of serious health problems.

"You miss **100%** of the shots you never take."

Wayne Gretzky, Canadian hockey player

What percentage of all fires occur in vehicles?

Roughly **20%** of all fires are car fires.

WHAT PERCENTAGE OF AMERICANS HAVE PRETENDED TO BE TALKING ON A CELL PHONE WHEN THERE WAS NO ONE ON THE OTHER END?

More people than you may think! **23%** of adults, **28%** of men, and **20%** of females have all used this trick to avoid talking to someone in front of them. Of these, **38%** are between the ages of eighteen and twenty-nine, **30%** are between the ages of thirty and thirty-nine, **13%** are between the ages of forty and forty-nine, **12%** are between the ages of fifty and sixty-four, and **6%** of these people are sixty-five or older. **18%** of married people have used the ploy compared to **30%** of unmarried people. Wow! It looks like Americans have an awful lot of people they would prefer to avoid!

What percentage of voters in the 2004 presidential election were unmarried?

36% were unmarried.

WHAT PERCENTAGE OF PEOPLE IN THE UNITED STATES HAVE MOBILE PHONES?

Almost **84%** of Americans use cell phones and this is likely to increase almost to **100%** in the next five years. While such widespread cell phone usage has its detractors—rude, mundane conversations, people letting their phones ring at the movies, in a restaurant, on a commuter train, etc.—cell phones really do keep us safer. The number of 911 calls has gone up **100%** to more than 50 million a year.

WHAT PERCENTAGE OF AMERICANS ARE WORRIED ABOUT ONLINE IDENTIFY THEFT?

60% of adult online shoppers are worried about their personal information being stolen. Nearly the same amount—**59%**—admit that they have had anxiety about their credit card information being swiped. Despite the concerns, consumers are increasingly shopping online—and online retailers are increasingly enticing them to do so. In an effort to increase sales, almost **72%** of online retailers upped the specials used to bring in online sales on Cyber Monday of this year.

HOW MANY AMERICAN CHILDREN ARE OVERWEIGHT?

Due to childhood favorites like chips, soda, and video games, **30%** of schoolchildren are overweight, and half that number—**15%**—are actually categorized as obese.

"90% of politics is deciding whom to blame. **"**

Meg Greenfield, U.S. journalist

WHAT PERCENTAGE OF CRIMES ARE WOMEN RESPONSIBLE FOR?

Surprisingly, women are responsible for **28%** of all property crimes and **15%** of all violent crimes. In recent years, female crimes have ballooned, increasing some **140%** since 1970 and show no signs of slowing down. Women account for high percentages of embezzlement (**41%**), fraud (**39%**), forgery (**36%**), and larceny-theft (**33%**). Also, women who are sent to prison for murder are twice as likely to have killed someone close to them like a boyfriend, child, or husband.

How many dogs travel with their owners on a family trip?

In 2002 only **16%** of dogs went along on the family vacation, but today, more than **19%** of pups are brought along for the ride.

By what percentage did the population of America grow between 1860 and 1910?

During the Civil War some 600,000 Americans lost their lives, but despite that and due to high rates of immigration from Southern and Eastern Europe and the East, the population of America grew by **300%**, from 31 million to more than 92 million people.

What percentage of communication is nonverbal?

Much more than you would think! **90%** of communication is actually not verbalized, but rather expressed through facial expression and body language. Studies have actually shown that women are more in tune with nonverbal communication than men. Ladies, keep that in mind the next time your husband can't pick up on your subtle—perhaps too subtle—hints.

What percentage of people drive to work and how long does the trip take them?

Forget about going green! A whopping **90%** of all commuters drive to work and, in **45%** of these cases, the commute takes less than twenty minutes. For **14%**, the commute lasts forty-five minutes or more.

What percentage of women are turned off by a man's dirty bedroom?

43% of women are truly disgusted by a messy man cave. **35%** feel that they need to teach their man how to clean. And **16%** are afraid that the mess will reflect negatively on them.

"When you have **7%** unemployed, you have **93%** working."

John Fitzgerald Kennedy, U.S. president

One might assume that the younger student might believe more than seniors—but one would be wrong. Only **23%** of younger college students have a general belief in paranormal concepts, but **31%** of college seniors and **34%** of graduate students believe in these ideas.

What percentage of women have ever poked their nose in their husband's e-mail?

67% of women admit to doing some online snooping while **33%** said they had done no such thing!

> Life is **10%** what you make it and **90%** how you take it.

Irving Berlin, American composer

88% believe in the Old Testament, **86%** believe in the New Testament, **33%** believe in the Torah, **9%** believe in the Koran, and **5%** believe in the Book of Mormon.

What is the favorite sexy kiss for women and men?

59% of women and **51%** of men said that they much preferred a slow and sensual kiss to something overly fast and brusque.

Is it possible to reduce a doctor's bill?

Experts say that you can reduce a doctor's bill simply by asking the doctor for a discount that is equal to the percentage your insurance doesn't pay. Hence, if you are asking for a reduction in the bill on Medicare, you'd ask for **20%** off. The likelihood of your doctor reducing the bill is quite good.

> **"50%** of life in the N.B.A. is sex. The other **50%** is money."
>
> Dennis Rodman, American basketball player

WHAT PERCENTAGE OF THE FAVORITES IN ALL THE KENTUCKY DERBY RACES ACTUALLY WON?

Only **37.5%** of those favored to win have actually won! The Kentucky Derby is famed for incredible upsets, and no one really knows who is going to win. The first upset at the Kentucky Derby occurred during the first race on May 17, 1875. A horse named Aristedes, who was to serve as a rabbit, surged into the lead and beat the favorite, Chesapeake, by a huge margin. Down through the years there have been many other memorable upsets. The greatest, odds-wise, was the 1913 race where a 90 to1 shot named Donerail, piloted by a jockey with the unusual name of Roscoe Goose, won.

How quickly do kids become addicted to cigarettes?

Shockingly, **10%** of kids who become addicted to smoking do so within two days of their first cigarette.

HOW MANY BIKES ARE STOLEN YEARLY?

With concerns about the environment and the price of gas fresh in everyone's minds, many Americans have started leaving their car keys at home and are using their bicycles to get where they need to go. Unfortunately, bikes are easy to steal and the owners of the 1.5 million bikes stolen every year can confirm this. In fact, sources claim that the FBI is made aware of only **34%** of what is actually stolen, making that number even higher. College students are often hit hard by this type of theft and have a **53%** chance of having their bicycle stolen during their time at school. Contributing to this trend is the fact that the profits made by selling stolen bikes have gone up **5%** in 2009 alone.

What percentage of Americans follow expiration dates?

Not as many as you would think. **40%** of Americans consume stale bread and **30%** eat canned goods after the expiration date. It gets worse! **33%** will eat anything that looks and smells OK. Not a good idea, according to the American Dietetic Association (ADA), that recommends throwing out milk seven days after it was bought, yogurt seven to ten days, and eggs three weeks after they land in your fridge.

What percentage of Americans approves of public surveillance cameras?

69% of the American public doesn't have a problem with Big Brother watching. Is that because we don't know how common this practice is? In our post–9/11 world, surveillance cameras are everywhere—malls, parking lots, airports, supermarkets, ATMs, traffic lights, etc. In fact, the chances of being caught on tape while you go about your daily routine add up to nearly **50%**.

How many people favor embryonic stem cell research?

70% of all adults favor embryonic stem cell research—which is being proven to greatly improve the lives of those living with conditions such as diabetes, multiple sclerosis, and spinal cord injury. This percentage includes **70%** of Catholics, **45%** of born-again Christians, **38%** of Evangelicals, and **51%** of those who consider themselves "very religious."

What is the riskiest download?

The riskiest download, surprisingly, is not pornography but rather musical downloads! **19.1%** of these downloads lead to sites that can load viral software into your computer, compromising your information and your privacy.

Who is happier in America—singles or married people?

64% of married people said they are currently living happily ever after, compared with only **43%** of singles.

What is the percentage of stay-at-home dads in the United States?

There are now 159,000 stay-at-home fathers, a figure that has risen **300%** in the last ten years! That's a long way from the oddball stay-at-home father figure celebrated in movies. But these men have a surprising problem, being shunned by stay-at-home moms. I guess being a good guy doesn't make you good company.

How much did the publication of books and magazines increase in the late nineteenth century?

Between 1880 and 1900, book publishing increased each year by **300%**.

How many men and women will be stalked?

8% of all American women and **2%** of all American men will be stalked during their lifetime—for a total of 1.4 million stalking victims every year. Most stalkers have been in relationships with the people they stalk, but many have never even met the victims or were just casual acquaintances.

HOW DANGEROUS IS THE HIPPO?

A lot more deadly than most people think it is! Some even go so far as to say that it is the most deadly animal on the planet. Anthropologist and animal writer Joseph Beck says that "on a scale of **1%** to **100%** I would put their dangerousness at **100%** with all other animals behind them." Hippos will readily attack human beings and even lunge after the boats that people are in.The hippo is certainly equipped to inflict massive, fatal damage. They have a huge mouth that, when open, displays teeth and tusks so daunting that one could easily understand how a hippo could cut a small boat in half with a single bite. Males normally weigh between 3,300 and 4,000 pounds and females between 1,900 and 3,300 pounds and they're surprisingly fast for all their bulk, capable of running up to thirty miles an hour, though not for long distances.

"I meant what I said, and I said what I meant. / An elephant's faithful, **100%**."

Dr. Seuss, U.S. author and illustrator

How much better is the Medicare drug plan given to Congressional employees than the standard drug plan?

Looks like Congressional employees luck out. The plan that they receive is actually **42%** better than the standard drug plan.

What percentage of the killer whale's diet is human?

Perhaps surprisingly, the answer is **0%**. Conceivably, killer or orca whales easily could dine on human beings, but it's just not in their nature. Rather, they are playful, intelligent, and highly trainable and feed on various animals in the wild including fish, sea lions, otters, and birds.

What percentage of Americans have totaled their parents' car?

Parent's of licensed drivers beware! A shocking **9%** of males and **4%** of females have totaled a parent's car! How very *Ferris Bueller's Day Off* of them!

WHAT PERCENTAGE OF AMERICANS SAY THEY HAVE A BETTER RELATIONSHIP WITH THEIR PARENTS NOW THAN THEY DID AS CHILDREN?

A whopping **89%** of people get along better with their parents now than they did when they were kids. A total of **88%** of women say this and **90%** of men. These percentages soar along with the income of the child. Only **79%** had a better adult relationship with Mom and Dad if their income was lower than $20,000, while out of households earning more than $100,000, **92%** believed that this was true.

WHAT IS THE PERCENTAGE OF PEOPLE WHO KEEP THEIR CELL PHONES ON ALL THE TIME?

49% of people keep their cell phones on all the time, even while they are asleep. This makes sense when you consider that more and more people are relying on their cell phones to function as their only phone. Oftentimes, a cell phone is cheaper and more convenient. The only drawback occurs when and if you are in an area where transmission and reception are poor.

WHAT INSTITUTIONS DO PEOPLE PUT THE MOST FAITH IN?

Most Americans put a great deal of faith in the military. In fact, **47%** put a great deal of confidence in the military, while **38%** have only some confidence, and only **14%** have hardly any.

After the military, **45%** of Americans put their faith in small business, followed by **38%** believing in colleges and universities, **33%** trusting the Supreme Court, **31%** trusting in medicine, **30%** in organized religion, **21%** in the courts and justice system, and **10%** in law firms.

> ## "Baseball is **90%** mental. The other half is physical."
>
> **Yogi Berra, U.S. baseball player**

How many popular songs contain references to sex and drugs?

33% of popular songs contain explicit references to sex and drugs while **42%** contain implicit mentions. Not surprisingly, **77%** of songs in the rap genre contain these references, and **36%** of all country music contains lyrics dealing with this type of material. The real shocker is the fact that rock songs only contain **14%** of these references. So much for sex, drugs, and rock 'n' roll!

HOW POPULAR IS ORGANIC FOOD?

Not nearly as popular as it once was. Since 2001, sales of organic food, driven by people's desire to eat food that doesn't contain pesticides and growth hormones, ballooned **150%** to reach sales of 19 billion in 2008, moving them from specialty food stores like Whole Foods to the produce aisles of Stop & Shop and Walmart. But, as living expenses have grown, organic popularity has waned. In today's tough economy, only **27%** of shoppers feel that buying organic is worth the extra money.

What percentage of people are grandparents?

Today, about **75%** of all adults over the age of sixty-five are grandparents. And it's estimated that about **50%** of today's grandparents will eventually become great-grandparents.

Which partner is more often the cause of infertility in a couple?

This responsibility is split right down the middle. **40%** of infertility issues are attributed to the man, and **40%** are attributed to the woman. The remaining **20%** are attributed to problems with both the man and woman or are unexplained. **25%** of all infertile couples have more than one factor that is causing their infertility.

At what age does the possibility of divorce decrease?

The possibility of divorce drops **24%** once the bride- or groom-to-be turns twenty-five years old. Maybe getting married right out of high school or college isn't the best idea!

HOW EFFECTIVE ARE BURGLAR ALARMS?

The reality of home alarms is quite different then the life-saving scenarios seen on TV commercials. Today, police are taking longer and longer to respond to alarms, sometimes up to a half hour or more. The problem is that many of the officers have developed a "Cry Wolf" mindset. All over the country, most alarms that come in are false due to mechanical flaws or an overly sensitive system, a pet triggering the alarm, or one of the worst culprits of all, an electrical storm. Typically, **99%** of burglary calls that come in are false alarms! In fact, many police departments have become so overwhelmed they have started fining homeowners and businesses. For example, last year the town of Kannapolis, North Carolina, recorded **99.3%** false alarms. As a result the Kannapolis city government started imposing fees, which ranged from $25 after the first couple of false alarms to $500 for repeat offenders.

If divorce has increased by **1000%**, don't blame the women's movement. Blame the obsolete sex roles on which our marriages were based.

Betty Friedan, U.S. feminist

What percentage of people in the United States live alone?

30.5 million people—or **27%** of all homeowners—live by themselves.

How effective is "the morning after pill" in preventing pregnancy?

Despite the controversial nature of the morning after pill, when such pills are used as emergency contraception, they reduce the risk of pregnancy by **75%** if they are started within three days of the unprotected intercourse. However, the pills can still work if the woman starts taking them up to five days after having unprotected sex.

HOW LONG CAN PEOPLE EXPECT TO LIVE?

In general, much longer than they used to. Today **48%** of men are expected to live to be eighty-five; **30%** are expected to live to be ninety; **25%** are expected to live to be ninety-five; and **5%** are expected to live to be 100. Women are expected to live even longer! **62%** of women are expected to live to be eighty-five; **42%** are expected to live to be ninety; **22%** are expected to live to be ninety-five; and **8%** are expected to live to be 100. There are various factors that go into these calculations. To get a free custom prediction, search online for a Longevity Calculator. One good one can be found at *www.wharton.upenn.edu*. Click on Wharton School, and then click on Mortality Calculator.

Can cleaning your car decrease your gas use?

Surprisingly yes! Cleaning 100 pounds of junk from your car can save you up to **2%** per miles per gallon.

"99% of who you are is invisible and untouchable."

Buckminster Fuller, American architect and author

What percentage of the time are psychics correct in their readings?

Some people, of course, are more gifted with psychic abilities than others. In tests conducted on students and professional psychics at the University of Arizona, it was found that, while ordinary students were able to psychically perceive things an average of **33%** of the time, professional psychics were able to perceive things well over **85%** of the time.

What are Americans doing with their fresh water?

Due to conservation efforts, water usage in the United States has decreased by **25%** since the 1970s. Today, **45%** of our water goes to industry; **42%** is used for agricultural purposes; only **13%** is used domestically.

How much of the world is drunk?

Roll out the barrel! It is estimated that, at any given time, **0.7%** of the population is half in the wrapper.

Does money make people happy?

Turns out the answer is yes! **72%** of those with incomes of $75,000 or higher report being very satisfied with their personal life, while a mere **36%** of those with an annual income of $30,000 or less were satisfied.

WHEN DO CHILDREN START WATCHING TELEVISION?

It's scary that by five months old, **40%** of all children have begun watching television. That percentage begins to look even more frightening when you take into consideration that children who begin watching TV at a young age end up with problems like aggression, lack of focus, and delayed cognitive skills. Despite these frightening percentages, most parents thought they were doing the right thing for their children. They considered the television to be:

Educational

Enjoyable and relaxing to watch

An electronic babysitter to entertain their kids while the parents were otherwise engaged

How many diets has the typical American tried?

27% of Americans say they've tried one or two diets. **23%** say they've tried more than five different diets, **18%** of people say they've tried three to five, and **11%** say that they are always dieting. On the other end of the spectrum, **21%** answered that they've never actually dieted.

WHAT'S THE BEST WAY FOR A GUY TO IMPRESS A GIRL?

Laughter and a good sense of humor matters most to the majority of women—**47%**! Many women will even date a man who is funny, although otherwise they wouldn't have looked twice at him. For **37%** of women, it is important that a date show that he has good manners and that he's a gentleman. Men, holding the door and allowing your lady to go first may get you further than you thought.

How dangerous is it to be a helicopter pilot in Iraq?

The percentage speaks for itself. More than **50%** of all helicopters involved in the war have been downed by enemy fire.

What percentage of people think it is a good idea to give the government access to their e-mail as a way to enhance national security?

Only **33%** believe this is a good idea with double that number—**66%**—strongly disagreeing.

What percentage of adults over the age of eighteen have gone skinny dipping?

Many people—**57%** of men and **38%** of women—have sampled this forbidden pleasure. Just make sure your clothes are still going to be there when you get out!

How much has home ownership increased since 1960?

Home ownership has increased by **10.2%** over the past thirty-plus years. Of course, due to predatory lending and rising foreclosure rates, we have learned that many buyers were sold homes they couldn't afford.

What percentage of Americans think women use PMS as an excuse to be grumpy?

The majority of people don't seem to think this way. Only **44%** of men and **37%** of females believe that women blame their crankiness on PMS. In general, out of people aged nineteen to twenty-nine, **51%** think women use this as an excuse, while only **31%** of people over sixty-five believe this.

Who is America's favorite TV star of the last twenty-five years?

Jerry Seinfeld won with **27%** of the vote. Johnny Carson came in second with **20%**, followed by Oprah Winfrey who received **18%**. Bill Cosby received **18%** of the vote and Michael J. Fox, **17%**.

What percentage of people believe in psychic powers?

Despite past skepticism, in recent years the percentage of those who believe has increased. Borne along by the popularity of such TV shows as *Medium* and superstar psychics like John Edward, **48%** of Americans now believe in psychic powers.

What foods can't you give up?

59% say they couldn't give up ice cream; **41%** couldn't give up potato chips if they tried; **51%** couldn't give up bread; and **29%** couldn't give up pasta. Perhaps most surprisingly—**52%** of Americans couldn't give up cheese versus only **48%** who are unable to give up chocolate.

How many children treated for acute lymphoblastic leukemia are cured?

This is the most common form of childhood cancer and 4,000 kids a year are diagnosed with it. Fortunately, today the cure rate is close to an astonishing **90%**! This is an amazing improvement over the cure rate of 1962, when only **4%** of children with this disease survived. The use of more effective drugs and more sophisticated genetic techniques used to personalize treatment have allowed for such great success.

WHAT IS IT LIKE TO BE A MILLIONAIRE?

A millionaire's lifestyle is not as glamorous as you may like to believe. We working folks tend to picture millionaires living a life of excess: fancy cars, designer clothes, private jets. Surprisingly, **60%** of millionaires drive not a Porsche or a Lamborghini, but an American-made car, and **50%** of millionaires have never spent more than $140 for a pair of shoes in their lives. Maybe they're millionaires because they're saving not spending? Something to keep in mind!

Which search engines are used most frequently?

Overall, 276 million Internet searches are done each month, and search engines like Google, Yahoo, and MSN are used to make **93%** of all these searches.

What percentage of Americans have a piercing where the sun doesn't shine?

9% of Americans have pierced themselves down under. Ouch!

How common are abortions?

Abortions are actually very common. In fact, more than **34%** of women in the United States will have an abortion by the time they are forty-five years old.

What percentage of lower income workers felt their jobs are now less safe due to terrorism?

20% of low-income workers feel like their jobs became more dangerous after the terrorist attacks on 9/11. People with incomes over $40,000 are **25%** more likely to say that their work got more dangerous, than were lower- and middle-income respondents.

"I have to go 150% or nothing at all."

Patti LaBelle, U.S. singer and actress

Which states produce the most wheat?

There are roughly 2.1 billion bushels of wheat—the essential ingredient of bread, rolls, pie crust, etc.—produced every year in the United States. Where does this wheat come from? Well, Kansas and North Dakota account for **28%** of the nation's wheat production.

WHAT PERCENTAGE OF KIDS PLAY VIDEO GAMES?

Are you really surprised that **97%** of kids spend their time playing video games? The numbers are pretty close as far as gender is concerned, with **99%** of boys and **94%** of girls playing. But there are scant differences along racial, ethnic, or income lines. Indeed, **7%** of the players said they didn't have a computer in their homes but did have a game console.

Of course the **97%** who play everyday and the games they play are as varied as their preferences in music or TV programs. **80%** of the players play five different games, with action, puzzles, racing, and sports most common. Some favorites include "Guitar Hero," "Madden's NFL" "Halo 3," and "Dance Dance Revolution."

Teens also obtain and play games that are rated "M" for Mature and "AO" for Adult. **75%** of the parents of game players say they check the ratings on the games at least sometimes. Perhaps parents are gilding the lily, because **50%** of boys cited an "AO" game as one of their favorites as opposed to only **14%** of young girls.

Interestingly, around **33%** of parents play video games with their kids all or some of the time.

> "It doesn't matter what part I play, I try and commit myself **100%**.
> Steve Buscemi, U.S. actor

Do most older drivers wear their seatbelts?

Thankfully, a large majority do! **75%** of older drivers wear their seat belts, compared to **62%** of other adult occupants (eighteen to sixty-four years old).

Which accessories are vital to make your life a beach?

48% believe that a cooler filled with cold drinks is the most important beach accessory. **32%** wouldn't dream of going to the beach without a comfortable chair, **17%** need a romance novel, and—bringing up the rear—**3%** long for a cute sarong.

What kinds of offenses are people in prison for?

In recent years, violent offenders account for **53%** of growth in the prison population, while those serving time for drug offenses account for **59%** of growth.

Are there still pawnshops in America and what do they charge?

Pawnshops certainly still exist in America, but they've changed their image. Many, instead of being sleazy dumps, are now spacious and well-lit, are located in malls, and cater to a wide variety of customers. It is estimated that **10%** of Americans will, at some point in their lives, do business at a pawnshop.

IS COFFEE GOOD FOR YOUR HEALTH?

It certainly appears that a cup of joe is good for women. Studies have confirmed that drinking two to three cups of coffee a day reduces a woman's chances of dying from heart disease by **24%**. Whether good or bad, coffee is definitely here to stay. Years ago, companies raised meat prices, and women stopped buying meat, forcing companies to lower the prices. A few years later they raised the price of coffee. What happened? Nothing.

BY WHAT PERCENTAGE HAS THE NUMBER OF SECULAR AMERICANS EXPANDED?

In recent years, the number of secularist Americans has expanded greatly. Today, the number of Americans who are not part of any formal religion has gone up more than **200%**. Overall, **16%** of Americans say that they have no links to formal religion. This group, while smaller than Evangelicals, includes scientists, journalists, and academics who are in the upper tiers of their professions and in a position to influence a disproportionate number of Americans with what they say.

HOW MUCH MORE WILL I PAY TO HAVE AN EXISTING ROOF REMOVED BEFORE A NEW ROOF IS INSTALLED?

You'll pay upward of **50%** more money for the roof removal, which isn't really necessary. You should not have the bad roof torn off unless it's so far gone that it's a hazard, or the town building code demands removal. Many town building departments will allow a second, or even a third, layer of roofing to be installed if it is determined that the framing can support the weight.

What percentage of Americans believe that an employer has the right to ask a female job candidate if she intends to become pregnant?

Overall, **18%** of Americans believe this question is fair game in a job interview. **12%** of men believe this is an appropriate question for an interviewer to ask.

Is marijuana more unhealthy than cigarette smoke?

Yes! Due to the fact that marijuana smoke contains **50%** to **80%** more carcinogens than regular cigarettes, it is more harmful both for the smoker and for the person breathing in the secondhand smoke. Marijuana smokers have a greater chance of contracting cancer as well as a greater risk of lung infection, among other more substantial respitory problems.

HOW MANY U.S. PARATROOPERS WERE EXPECTED TO SURVIVE D-DAY?

There is a famous picture of Supreme Allied Commander Dwight D. Eisenhower shaking hands and speaking with members of the 101st Airborne, who were the first Allied troops to invade German-held territory on D-Day. It is amazing that one doesn't see tears in Eisenhower's eyes because he fully expected that **80%** of the men would be killed. Prognosticators were wrong, and **60%** of the 101st Airborne survived.

> Life is a sexually transmitted disease and the mortality rate is **100%.**
>
> R. D. Laing, Scottish Psychologist

What percentage of Africa is uninhabited by humans?

28% of Africa remains uninhabited and unsettled.

What are the most popular pets in America?

Americans sure do love their animals! **63%** of all households—that's 69 million households!—own a pet. 73 million Americans are experiencing puppy love and 90 million Americans are cozying up with their cats. 139 million Americans take care of freshwater fish and 9 million Americans take care of saltwater fish. In addition, we own 16 million birds, 18 million small animals, and 11 million reptiles.

Love and companionship drive the desire to care for other creatures, and **59%** of pet owners also feel that pets are beneficial to health.

Is living with a smoker dangerous?

It sure is! Breathing in secondhand smoke raises one's risk of contracting lung cancer by **11%**! It also raises the risk of contracting breast cancer by a whopping **68%**.

"And will you succeed? Yes! You will indeed! (98.75% guaranteed)."

Dr. Seuss,
U.S. author and illustrator

WHAT PERCENTAGE OF VOTERS WOULD VOTE FOR A CANDIDATE DESPITE DISAGREEING ON VOLATILE ISSUES?

Some people draw their line in the sand at different issues. **51%** of Americans would not vote for a candidate if he or she disagreed with their stance on abortion, while **49%** could. Voters were split down the middle on the issue of gay marriage as well. **55%** would not vote for a candidate who disagreed with them, while **45%** could. On stem cell research, voters were split **50%** to **50%**.

What percentage of Americans will be self-employed?

It seems like a large number of Americans don't work well with others. Up to **40%** of the U.S. population will, at some point in their lives, be self-employed.

HAVE AIR TRAVEL COMPLAINTS INCREASED?

They surely have. In 2007 there were 13,168 complaints, up a whopping **58%** from 2006. The reason, in general, seems to be that pilots, airline personnel, and passengers are subject to search and that, combined with the fear of terrorism and the increased cost of flying, has created a much more stressful environment for all. In 2007, **34%** of consumers complained about the flights themselves, **22%** about baggage problems, **11%** about reservation tickets and boarding, **10%** about customer service, and **11%** about fares and discrimination.

WHAT PERCENTAGE CAN YOU GET OFF RETAIL ITEMS IN SPRINGTIME?

Ah, springtime! Chirping birds, blooming plants, and amazing sales! In April, you can find Easter candy for up to **75%** off! Trust me, chocolate tastes just as good, maybe even better, when it's on sale!

In May, keep an eye out for sales on gardening supplies, luggage, mattresses, outdoor furniture, and TVs and other appliances. May is also a good time to travel at discount prices. Since it is just before the peak summer months, you will find most facilities open but with prices as much as **40%** less than what you might pay in another month. You'll also have a more enjoyable time with fewer crowds!

How many volcanoes does Japan have?

Japan, as an archipelago, was born from volcanoes. Therefore, it's not surprising to realize that it has approximately 200 volcanoes and is home to **10%** of the active volcanoes in the world.

WHAT PERCENTAGE OF BOTTLED WATER COMES FROM SPRINGS?

75% of bottled water comes from natural springs and the like, but a shocking **25%** comes from various city and town water supplies. This water—which is normally free from our taps—has been treated and purified and sold to us at a greatly increased price. Until relatively recently, water bottlers were not required to state the water source on their label, but this is changing. Aquafina is going to begin stating that its water comes from municipal sources; NestlePure will state whether the water comes from deep well sources or public sources; Dasani acknowledges on its website that its water come from local water sources. So how were you fooled? Simple, water bottle labels often show pictures of mountains, tall pine trees, and bubbling brooks. But these pictures are meaningless. If the label does not specifically state that the source is spring water, you should be suspicious.

WHAT PLAYERS HAVE THE HIGHEST BATTING AVERAGES SINCE BASEBALL WAS LAUNCHED IN 1876?

The best hitters are normally decided by who has the best batting average—the number of hits the player has divided into the number of times the player had an at bat. By that standard, the best hitter ever is Ty Cobb, who had a lifetime batting average of .366, or a hit around **36%** of the time he came to bat. Next are Roger Hornsby, who batted .358, Joe Jackson (who was depicted in the hit film *Field of Dreams*) who hit .356, Ed Delahanty who hit .346 and the incomparable Ted Williams who hit .344, over his lifetime. Why were these men such great hitters? This is probably due to their great reflexes, and their ability to see the ball clearly as it sped toward home plate.

How macho is too macho?

81% of young women want their man to be a little tough—and also somewhat jealous. **15%** said they wouldn't want to date anyone who was either tough or jealous. They think that type of a man is embarrassing. Finally, **3%** of all women wanted a boyfriend whose macho demeanor matched that of Al Pacino in the movie *Scarface*.

What percentage of Americans believe in Heaven?

75% of Americans believe in some sort of an afterlife. However, there aren't any numbers available as to how many Americans believe they have a shot at getting Saint Peter to open up those pearly gates!

Do your husband's eating habits impact the way you eat?

70% of women said their husband's habits don't impact what they put on the plate at all.

WHAT PERCENTAGE OF TEENS HAVE HAD SOME TYPE OF SEXUAL EXPERIENCE?

Today, roughly **50%** of all teens have had some type of sexual experience. Thankfully, this percentage has decreased since the 1990s. There are a variety of things that may have caused this decrease. One reason may be the fear of AIDS—this is the first generation that this disease has hovered over. Additionally, for girls, becoming pregnant has become less socially acceptable and the Internet gives steady access to a ream of information on sex so teens are better informed and therefore make better choices. Some of these sites show the birthing process in detail and drive teen girls away by fear of the consequences of pregnancy as much as anything else.

Has the family dinner gone the way of the dodo bird?

It seems like the time-honored tradition of family dinner is alive and well in America. **57%** of all children under six years old sit down every night to bond with their parents over dinner. In addition, **24%** of kids eat breakfast with their parents on a daily basis.

WHEN WAS THE GREATEST NUMBER OF BABIES BORN IN AMERICA DURING THE 20TH CENTURY?

More babies were born in the 1960s than in any other decade in the 20th century. The baby boom between 1946 and 1964 produced 78 million babies, a number that other periods in the century could hardly match. And almost **64%** of these babies were born before 1960. These babies will account for **28%** of the American population in 2030 when the youngest of them will turn 66 and the oldest 84.

How many non-U.S. citizens are in U.S. prisons?

About **4%** of prison inmates are not U.S. citizens.

What percentage of senior citizens are interested in who wins the Oscars?

22% of people over sixty have little or no interest, and **36%** say that they're not sure who will win the Oscars this year, which could well indicate a lack of interest!

What percentage of people don't pay income tax?

Around **33%** or 42,500,000 people in the United States are not required to pay any tax each year.

❝ I support the president 100%—when he's right. ❞ Richard Shelby, U.S. politician

What is the sun made up of?

The sun, made exclusively of gases, is **75%** hydrogen and **25%** helium by mass.

What percentage of people regret having sex in high school?

Up to **66%** of people who lost their virginity in high school regret it. Many high schoolers want to swipe their V-card before they head off for college, but they are conflicted by society telling them to wait for things like love and marriage. This confusion can result in these students feeling confused about sex, which may cause them to regret their decision.

How is preventive medicine regarded in America?

49% of Americans believe that preventive care is the answer to the majority of health problems, but only **46%** of those Americans know how to achieve it.

WHEN CAN YOU SAVE MONEY ON SUMMER CLOTHES?

July and August are the best times to invest in summer clothes for next year. July marks the end of the summer and warm weather season for stores that need to start getting ready for the back-to-school season. This is a great time to buy heavily discounted bathing suits and beachwear. Store brand clothing often goes on sale at drastic discounts—you can save more than **80%** at some stores—during this time period. A number of large items also can go on sale in July. Look for: air conditioners, appliances, audiovisual equipment, furniture, bicycles, mattresses, refrigerators, tires, and washers and dryers.

Do companies care if their customers leave them?

They surely do. On average, if a business is able to hang on to an extra **5%** of its customers, their profits increase by an average of **44%**.

How do doctors feel about pills that greatly reduce the number of periods a woman experiences in a year?

Some people are concerned that suppressing menstruation can be harmful and goes against nature. However, **97%** of doctors are not opposed to the concept and believe the drugs to be safe and effective.

CAN YOU ADOPT A WILD ANIMAL?

Yes. You can symbolically adopt an animal at **75%** of the nation's zoos or online at *www.worldwildlife.org*. In other words, you pay an "adoption" fee and receive a photo and information about the animal. Obviously, you don't get to bring a polar bear home with you! Sometimes the size of the animal you can adopt depends on the size of your donation. For example, you may pay less to adopt a lovebird than you would to adopt an elephant. If you have a zoo nearby, call them and ask about their adoption programs. For your donation, many zoos allow free admission on certain days.

At least one person didn't get the memo about not being able to raise a wild animal in his home. A man in New York raised a Bengal tiger to full-grown size in his apartment in Harlem. One of the most memorable photos ever was the sight of the tiger looking out a double hung window; its head filled half of it. The same man also kept a small alligator in another room.

> **We still do not know .0001% of what nature has revealed to us.**
>
> Albert Einstein, German-born physicist

What percentage can you get off on your healthcare costs?

In the case of doctors, dentists, and pharmacists **56%** of people ask for whatever their insurance company won't cover. If you go into the hospital and ask the chief financial officer for a percentage off, you may get a **30%** discount, but you have to ask for it.

What percentage of fights did Rocky Marciano win?

Rocky Marciano, world heavyweight champion, won **100%** of the time! He won all of his forty-nine fights and defended his title six times.

How many criminals were drinking when they broke the law?

Of the millions of people arrested each year, about **36%** were estimated to have been drinking at the time they committed their crime. The vast majority of these alcohol-involved offenders are sentenced to supervised community service.

What percentage of Americans own a firearm?

30% of Americans admit to owning a gun. It's the other **70%** that we have to watch out for!

How many people living in America are foreign-born?

Roughly **12.6%** of the U.S. population is made up of individuals who were not born in America.

What percentage of Americans have been diagnosed with diabetes?

23.6 million people or **7.8%** of the population have been diagnosed with diabetes—and this number is expected to continue to increase.

What percentage of Americans think added airport security has made a difference in thwarting terrorist attacks?

59% of Americans believe the strengthened airport security has made a terrorist attack less likely.

HOW MANY MURDERS GO UNSOLVED?

You would think that with DNA testing and the detailed forensic information available today that every homicide would be solved. Unfortunately, this is not the case. Roughly **39%** of all homicides go unsolved yearly. There are various reasons why people get away with murder; lack of police training and the mishandling of evidence are among the most common. While close to **61%** of murders are solved, they are mostly simple investigations—like when a family member kills a family member. A "whodunit"—any case that goes forty-eight hours or more unsolved—is a lot more difficult to close.

The one good thing about a homicide investigation is that the statute of limitations never runs out. Society frowns on people who murder other people and the perps are subject to investigation and arrest for as long as they live.

"When I take a picture I take **10%** of what I see."

Annie Leibovitz, U.S. photographer

How many prisoners receive parole?

At least **95%** of all prisoners are released from prison at some point and nearly **80%** percent are paroled.

How many scientists don't believe in the paranormal?

96% of scientists describe themselves as "skeptical" of extra sensory perception or ESP, although **2%** believe in PSI—a combination of ESP and psychokinesis—and **10%** feel that parapsychological research should be encouraged.

"I'm really **95%** Mr. Rogers, and only **5%** Oscar the Grouch."

George Steinbrenner

What percentage of the day do Americans think about their race?

African Americans think about their race **52%** of the day, more than twice the amount of Asian Americans who think about race **25%** of the time. Hispanics think about their race **24%** of the day, which is more than six times more frequently than Caucasians who think about race **8%** of the time.

What percentage of school-age children smoke marijuana?

The numbers are shocking! Roughly **38.4%** of high school students report using marijuana at some point while in high school. **16.5%** of eighth graders, **34.1%** of tenth graders, and **44.8%** of twelfth graders reported marijuana use.

What percentage of people are night owls?

37% of people are early birds; **41%** are night owls; **21%** fall somewhere in between on that spectrum. However, it's not always that easy to put people in various pigeonholes. For example, not all early birds get up early by choice. Many simply have to get up early to work.

What percentage of the population suffers from ice cream headaches?

We've all experienced the ice cream headache, right? You go to the freezer, scoop out a big bowl of your favorite frozen treat, take a big bite, and . . . suddenly experience a horrific, shooting pain! Well, unfortunately for the **33%** of you who have suffered through this experience, you're in the minority. Most people can shovel ice cream, slurpees, and popsicles down their throat without a single wince!

" Let's face it, **80%** of the work I do my kids can't see,"

Joe Pantoliano, American actor

What percentage of cats and dogs have health insurance?

This percentage is small, but is increasing daily. Right now, **3%** of dogs and **1%** of cats are insured in the United States. The concept of pet insurance began in Europe and today **20%** of English pets are insured compared to **49%** of Swedish pets.

How many people support Medicaid?

91% of all adults support the use of Medicaid, which provides health insurance to those living on very low incomes.

What professionals do Americans trust most?

83% of Americans hold nurses in the highest regard. Grade school teachers came in a close second at **74%**; pharmacists came in third at **71%**; military officers came in fourth at **65%**.

What percentage of people consider themselves to be religious?

21% of Americans identify themselves as very religious, **19%** as not very religious, **12%** as religious not at all, and **48%** as somewhat religious.

What percentage of women are upset when the guy they're with checks out other females?

61% of females said they weren't bothered when their man's eyes strayed, unless it was more than a glance. **27%** said it doesn't bother them because they knew guys can't help but look, but **11%** don't like it at all and said the guy should keep his eyes on them.

How many stalking victims were cyber-stalked?

25% of all victims experienced some kind of online harassment, with **83%** of them being contacted via e-mail.

IS IT TRUE THAT VULTURES ARE ALMOST EXTINCT?

In the past few years, **95%** of the vultures in Pakistan and India have died. You would think that a bird whose everyday meals consist of a variety of carcasses ranging from elephants to cows would thrive, but indeed they are not. Normally, when cattle or other livestock died, farmers would just wait for the vultures to come around and strip the carcass. But cattle farmers have recently begun giving their livestock a new chemical to help them live longer, which is taking away a main source of food and decimating the vulture population.

> "I'd guess that **80%** of the people who work for Playboy are feminists."
>
> Christie Hefner, former CEO of Playboy Enterprises

WHAT PERCENTAGE OF EMPLOYERS BELIEVE HIGH SCHOOL GRADUATES LACK READING SKILLS?

38% of employers would like to see high school graduates with higher reading levels. The reason behind this inability to read well is that people are reading for pleasure a lot less, and this covers a wide spectrum of reading material including magazines, newspapers, books, and online. Studies show that people who don't read are less likely to be successful at work and are also less likely to be involved in civil life.

What percentage of people back universal health coverage?

75% percent of all adults believe that everyone has a right to health care. This number includes more than **63%** of all religious group members.

How many Americans work off the books?

This is obviously a difficult figure to come by. Not everyone goes around bragging to the world about how they have beaten the IRS, but it is estimated that close to **5%** work off the books. This, of course, translates into millions of lost tax dollars. It is a wonder that the IRS doesn't start a campaign to collect those taxes!

How long will it take for termites to tear down your house?

A long, long time! It takes termites about five years to create a mature colony that can then disperse and make new colonies. Termites also eat slowly and not that much. A mature colony of 250,000 termites, for example, only consumes about one standard 2" x 4" x 8" board a year—which adds up to be way less than even **1%** of a house.

What percentage of inmates are injured in prison?

About **50%** of state inmates who served six or more years said they had been injured after confinement, while less than **20%** of those who had been in prison for less than two years reported an injury.

HOW MANY PEOPLE READ THE PRODUCT WARRANTIES THEY PURCHASE?

Close to **42%** of people do not even take the time to look at the extended warranty policies that come with their purchase. Furthermore, **46%** do not bother to read their service contracts. Extended warranties and service contracts are popular with consumers and can be very profitable for retailers. Generally, the profit margin on these products is slim, but this margin increases by **50%** to **60%** once an extended warranty is purchased.

WHAT PERCENTAGE OF PEOPLE WHO USE PSYCHICS WANT TO FIND OUT IF A DECEASED INVIDIVUAL IS ALRIGHT?

People, of course, have believed in the psychic for a long time. In fact, Abraham Lincoln's wife, Mary Todd Lincoln, tried to communicate with her dead son psychically. When a person goes to a psychic to try to communicate with someone who is deceased, there are many reasons for this communication. However, **90%** of the time, the living person simply wants to determine if their loved one is all right.

Are roadside diners becoming extinct?

At their peak, there were over 6,000 roadside diners in the United States. Today, those numbers have declined to 2,500—an almost **42%** drop. However, it's unlikely that they will go away completely. They have an ally in The American Diner Museum, a Rhode-Island–based nonprofit organization that has been in operation since 1996 and is devoted to preserving the roadside diner as an important piece of Americana.

HOW DANGEROUS ARE BIRD STRIKES (COLLISION WITH BIRDS)?

Bird strikes are very dangerous. For example in 1995 an Air Wacs E 3 plane collided with a flock of thirty geese which brought the plane down and resulted in all twenty-four crew members aboard being killed. But very few people know how frequent these strikes are because the FAA declines to release whatever information they have, and reporting a bird strike is not mandatory. Experts maintain that only **20%** of all bird strikes are reported.

Fortunately, the latest bird strike had a happy ending when the heroic pilot and crew were able to bring the 310 Jet down onto the Hudson River after the craft, US Airways Flight 549, lost both engines in a collision with birds.

IF THE ACADEMY AWARDS WERE HELD TODAY, WOULD THE WINNERS OF YEARS GONE BY STILL BE WINNERS?

Unfortunately for most winners, they wouldn't receive their Oscars if the votes were retabulated using today's numbers.

In 1998, *Shakespeare in Love* won an Oscar for best picture. If this vote were refigured today, *Saving Private Ryan* would take home the trophy with **44%** of the vote, versus *Shakespeare in Love*'s **23%**.

In 2003, Renee Zellweger won a Best Supporting Actress Oscar for her role in *Cold Mountain*. If the vote were refigured, Shohreh Aghdashloo would be the recall winner for *House of Sand and Fog* with **27%** of the votes, over Zellweger who would only receive **12%**.

What percentage of same-sex, unmarried-partner households include children?

39% of unmarried, same-sex households include children.

How much have cable companies raised their rates?

The problem with cable companies is that they have managed to become the only game in town. Due to this monopoly, cable rates have gone up **93%** during the past few years.

"99% of all failures come from people who have the habit of making excuses.**"**

George Washington Carver, U.S. educator and chemist

How many children under the age of two watch TV every day?

An astonishing **43%**!

HOW MANY OWNERS SPOIL THEIR PETS ROTTEN?

This trend is on the upswing and more and more cats and dogs are living the good life. Owners are doling out gifts like gift-giving is going out of style. **80%** of dog owners give their dogs gifts and **63%** of cat owners do the same for their furry felines. In addition to Christmas, Chanukah, and pet birthday parties, many owners are also giving gifts on such offbeat holidays as Easter and Halloween. Owners are also spreading the puppy love around on Valentine's Day. Owners spend an average of $17 per gift.

HOW GREAT IS THE CALORIC PERCENTAGE THAT ONE BURNS USING THE TECHNIQUE KNOWN AS NORDIC WALKING?

Nordic walking, where you use special poles that help you walk on asphalt, sand, grass, snow, or dirt allows you to burn **20%** to **40%** more calories than if you were walking normally. The technique involves long strides and flowing arm movements. Also, although it's possible to learn the technique on your own, and most poles come with an instructional DVD, it might be a good idea to take a course to perfect the technique. Health clubs and sporting good stores can help you locate someone to help.

WHAT PERCENT OF KIDS MISS SCHOOL DUE TO ANXIETY?

There are a variety of different kinds of anxiety that fall under the general umbrella term. Separation anxiety is most common in younger children and involves those children not wanting to leave a parent. Social anxiety and performance anxiety involve the student worrying about what others think of them, or how others will perceive them. At any rate, between **2%** and **5%** of students miss school due to some form of anxiety.

WHAT PERCENTAGE OF WOMEN HAVE EXPERIENCED POSTPARTUM DEPRESSION?

"Baseball was 100% of my life."

Ty Cobb, U.S. baseball player

Many women have mood swings right after they deliver their babies and can have difficulty sleeping, and feel somewhat depressed. If these symptoms begin a few days after delivery and go away after seven to ten days without treatment, they are likely indicative of "baby blues," a temporary condition that **50%** to **80%** of women feel, and which usually doesn't require medical attention.

Postpartum depression is a more serious situation and usually requires mental health care and/or prescription medication. Postpartum depression affects roughly **10%** to **15%** of women any time from a month to a year after childbirth.

What percentage of Americans are farmers?

Perhaps less than you'd think. Today, less than **1%** of Americans are full-time farmers, which is quite different from the late nineteenth century when **25%** of the population earned their living through agriculture.

What percentage of American births are to women who are separated, widowed, divorced, or never married?

35% of American births fit into this category.

HOW DO PEOPLE PREPARE FOR BED?

It is recommended that people prepare for bedtime by partici-pating in a soothing activity—reading, taking a bath, etc.—that transitions them from being awake to being ready for bed. Sex is also recommended as a great sleep inducer, although **44%** of middle-age women say they don't have time. The majority of people bypass sleep preparation and women are prime offend-ers. **21%** of women spend the last hour or so before bedtime catching up on work or paperwork; **36%** are on the Internet; **37%** take care of their children; a whopping **60%** catch up on household chores.

What is the secret to becoming a millionaire?

A money-making idea that many millionaires swear by is to always pay yourself first when you have money coming in. In other words, before paying bills or doing anything else, be sure to put **10%** away for yourself. In time that **10%** will add up and you'll be on your way to the Forbes top 100.

HOW MANY CHINESE CHILDREN ARE OVERWEIGHT?

There are kids in America who struggle with their weight, but there are also kids in China who are categorized as obese, albeit not as many. Only **10%** of Chinese children are obese, but this percentage is increasing by **8%** a year. **14.8%** of boys in primary schools are obese and in addition to this, another **13.2%** are overweight. **9%** of girls are obese with **11%** more overweight. In big cities such as Shanghai and Beijing, **20%** of children are obese, no doubt because of easier access to junk food. Hoping to turn this rising trend around, Chinese officials have alerted people to the dangers of obesity, such as diabetes, high blood pressure, noninfectious chronic diseases, and a decrease in mental function.

WHY IS TURKEY AN IMPORTANT ORNITHOLOGICAL ROUTE?

Out of the nearly 10 billion migratory birds on Earth, 1 billion—**10%**—travel through Turkey, which is the gateway for birds traveling to Europe and Africa. There are 450 species of birds living in Turkey out of 8,000 species worldwide, but **66%** of these Turkish birds are migratory. These flocks of birds never get lost and always manage to find their way home by using insoluble signs such as rivers and mountains as their roadmap.

HOW MUCH WEIGHT DO LENDERS PUT IN THE FACTORS THAT MAKE UP A CREDIT REPORT?

Banks believe that the biggest factor is the way you pay—this makes up **35%** of your credit score. **30%** is given to your existing credit, **15%** is given to the length of your credit history, **10%** is given to the types of credit you hold, and **10%** is given to the number of inquiries regarding your credit by lenders, landlords, credit card companies, etc.

What percentage of people believe that the mind can heal the body?

This idea is becoming more relevant in American society as even doctors are beginning to believe in the possibility of mind over matter. In fact, more than half of Americans—**55%** in fact—believe this, and cite the way placebos have worked on the body as empirical evidence.

What twenty-game winning major league pitcher holds the record for the highest winning percentage?

Ron Guidry, "Louisiana Lightning," went 25–3 for a **89.3%** win record in 1978 while pitching for the New York Yankees. Guidry was the American League Cy Young Award winner that year and finished second in MVP voting.

What areas in America have seen the greatest population gains?

During the 1990s the population of Nevada jumped **66%**, the greatest gain in the nation. Arizona vaulted **40%**, and the populations of Utah and Colorado both went up **30%**. It is predicted that these areas will continue to mushroom in size at an even quicker clip. By 2030 Nevada and Arizona are expected to increase their populations by another **50%**.

What percentage of troops experience serious mental problems resulting from their tours in Iraq?

An astonishing **30%** of all U.S. troops have suffered serious mental problems, including post-traumatic stress disorder, within three to four months after returning home.

Some 7.5 million adults suffer from dementia, but physicians say that, out of those millions, some 375,000 people may actually have a curable condition called normal pressure hydrocephalus or NPH. NPH affects the blood supply to the brain, which causes dementia-like symptoms such as difficulty walking, loss of bladder control, and slower thinking. Following surgery, between **85%** and **90%** of NPH sufferers show improvement, but there are potential complications such as clots, infection, and seizures. However, most people would consider it worth the risk.

What percentage of people in the United Kingdom prefer to die at home?

Roughly, only **4%** of British people want to die in the hospital, with the majority—**64%**—wishing to die in their own home. Right now those wishes are not being fulfilled; only **25%** of Brits with cancer die at home. However, the British House of Commons is campaigning for all people to have the choice of hospice care for their last days.

Which goody two-shoes celebrity would you most want to corrupt?

13% would want to corrupt Kelly Clarkson, **19%** Amanda Bynes, **30%** Hilary Duff, and **38%** Mandy Moore.

What percentage does sexual desire increase following breast augmentation surgery?

Following breast augmentation surgery, women have increased self-esteem, in addition to an increased sex drive. For a majority of women, sexual desire increased by a whopping **81%**!

How accurate are colonoscopy retesting reports?

No one argues that you shouldn't get a colonoscopy, but how often should you have one? Unfortunately, **65%** of all colonoscopy reports incorrectly state when retesting should occur. This means that more and more people with a low risk of colon cancer are being tested more frequently, making it more difficult for those high-risk people to schedule an appointment.

" I'm trying not to put myself into anything I'm not **100%** confident about. "

Christian Slater, American actor

What American city has the highest percentage of African American citizens?

African Americans make up **13.4%** of the total American population, and Detroit—with **84%** of the population—is the city with the most African American citizens.

How much income do retail stores lose to shoplifters each year?

Retail stores suffer an annual inventory loss of roughly **1.7%** per year. That may seem small, but in fact stores lose millions and millions of dollars every year due to stolen merchandise. Oftentimes, stores try to cover this loss by increasing their prices—hurting your wallet in turn.

What percentage of Americans own or plan to own an e-reader?

Only **3%** of Americans currently own an e-book reader and **80%** report that they have no plans to purchase one any time in the near future!

What areas of the United States contain the most native-born people—in other words, people who never moved away?

Roughly **80%** of the U.S.-born population of Louisiana and New York was born in those states (**82.2%** and **82.1%**, respectively). At the other end of the spectrum, only **28.5%** of the U.S.-born population living in Nevada was born there.

What percentage of Iraqi citizens don't have access to an adequate water supply?

Roughly **70%** of all citizens of Iraq are lacking an adequate, clean water source.

Will driving less result in reduced premiums from insurance companies?

It can. Many insurance companies offer low-mileage discounts of **10%** or more for drivers who motor fewer that 7,500 miles a year due to their decreased chance of getting into an accident. Some companies will even shave premiums by **5%** to **30%** per year for drivers who have been accident-free for five years.

What percentage of men have had something confiscated at the airport?

20% have fumed at airport security when their property was confiscated.

Does it pay to move yourself instead of hiring a moving company?

It surely does! By moving yourself you can save between **30%** and **80%**. Rent your own truck or trailer, find used boxes, convince your friends to help you out, and get ready to work your muscles. The only problem with this scenario is that you have to move all those boxes!

"When one bases his life on principle, **99%** of his decisions are already made."

Unknown

WHAT PERCENTAGE OF PEOPLE GET THEIR HEALTH IN-FORMATION ONLINE?

58% of Americans head online to figure out what is wrong with them health-wise, but those who go this route have to be very careful. Some of the information given—perhaps a lot of it—is simply wrong because the writer is not careful in his or her research, bad facts are repeated rather than checked out, and sometimes the writer's self interest outweighs a desire to speak the truth.

WHAT PERCENTAGE OF PEOPLE BELIEVE IN GHOSTS AND OTHER PARANORMAL ENTITIES?

Over half of the people in America—**51%**—believe in ghosts. **58%** of women hold this belief, compared to **42%** of men. Age also matters. **65%** of all people who are between the ages of twenty-five and twenty-nine believe in ghosts, while only **17%** of people over sixty-five believe in them. In addition, **33%** of Americans believe in such things as astrology; **27%** believe in reincarnation—which is where a person comes back after death with another identity; and **34%** believe in UFOs.

> "A telephone survey says that **51%** of college students drink until they pass out at least once a month. The other **49%** didn't answer the phone."
>
> Craig Kilborn, U.S. comedian

How many part-time workers are there?

There are now 25 million part-time workers—twice as many women as men—and now **36%** of employers give employees the opportunity to work part-time. **46%** of employers permit job sharing; **31%** of employers offer flex time, and **39%** allow telecommuting. It is also generally conceded that hiring part-time employees instead of full-time workers results in a lessening of service, because part-timers, in general, simply don't care as much as full-timers.

What country spends the most money on their military?

The world spends a lot on their military, over $1 trillion per year collectively. The United States is responsible for **46%** of that world total, followed far behind by Britain, France, Japan, and China, who are responsible for between **4%** and **5%** each.

Do you have to actually hear a joke to benefit from laughter?

No, you don't. Just anticipating a joke can reduce your level of stress by up to **70%**.

What percentage of people will regret something they ate during the course of the day? **32%** will rue that jelly donut, side of French fries, or bowl of ice cream.

Do American drivers keep their tires properly inflated?

27% of cars and **32%** of light trucks are driven with at least one or more under-inflated tires. Under-inflated tires wear badly and, in fact, drivers could reduce the cost of tire replacement by **50%** simply by adding a little air.

❝ A successful book cannot afford to be more than **10%** new. ❞

Marshall McLuhan, Canadian educator, philosopher, and scholar

HOW ACCURATE ARE HEART STRESS TESTS?

There are two types of heart stress tests. The first, an echocardiogram or ECG test is accurate in around **70%** of the cases. The chemical type of test is called a thallium or technetium scan. With this test, radioactive thallium (which is not dangerous) is given to the patient, and images are taken of the heart by highly sophisticated cameras to see how the blood is flowing. This test is accurate **85%** to **95%** of the time.

How many people would confront their spouses if they thought they were cheating?

While cheating can be extremely damaging to a relationship, **50%** of men and women said they would confront their spouses about infidelity and try to save the marriage.

"If marriages were made by putting all the men's names into one sack and the women's names into another, and having them taken out by a blindfolded child like lottery numbers, there would be just as high a percentage of happy marriages as we have here in England. . . . If you can tell me of any trustworthy method of selecting a wife, I shall be happy to make use of it."

George Bernard Shaw, Anglo-Irish playwright

What percentage of men could benefit from instruction on how to please a woman?

One New York psychiatrist estimates that between **75%** and **80%** could benefit. Women want to feel valued during lovemaking and many men just don't understand the emotional makeup of a woman—or how this comes into play in the bedroom.

WHAT PERCENTAGE OF ELECTRICAL DEVICES DRAW ENERGY EVEN WHEN THEY ARE TURNED OFF?

Many electrical devices draw electricity even when they have been turned off. Called the standby mode by the industry and "vampire" energy suckers by critics, these devices consume a ton of electricity, even though you may not realize it. For this reason the Energy Star program adopted a standard that would cut this energy use dramatically. As a result, you'll find Energy Star ratings for home electronics such as cordless phones, TVs, DVDs, battery charging systems, and home audio. If all of these devices in your home met the Energy Star standard, you would save about **75%** on energy costs per year.

What percentage of smokers would like to quit?

In our health-conscious country, **81%** of current smokers say they would like to quit smoking. **79%** say that they're addicted to smoking, which would make it hard to stop.

WHAT IS THE SHORTEST TIME AN ACTRESS WHO WAS NOMINATED FOR A BEST SUPPORTING ACTRESS OSCAR AWARD WAS ON SCREEN IN A FILM?

An actress named Maria Ouspenskaya was in the film *Dodsworth* for only **5%** of the film and Talia Shire was in the *Godfather II* for only **6%** of the time. On the other side of the spectrum, Cate Blanchett who was in *Notes on a Scandal* in 2006 was on screen for **63%** of the film's duration, and Mary Badham of *To Kill A Mockingbird* fame was on screen for a total of **68%** of the film.

> " Luck is what you have left over after you give **100%**. "
>
> Langston Coleman

JUST HOW MUCH DO DOG OWNERS CARE ABOUT THEIR DOGS?

Dog owners care tremendously about their pups. Dogs add a tremendous amount of joy to peoples' lives, and owners care deeply about them, something they demonstrate by their actions. For example:

30% of all dog owners carry a picture of their dog in their wallets.

25% of owners have missed work because of their dog's illnesses.

46% of owners who do not have a doggie door, open their doors for their pets at least a dozen times a day.

Who controls the sale of diamonds worldwide?

DeBeers controls **98%** of all diamonds, and they put them out at the price they wish. Diamonds are actually not the world's rarest stone, but they have been brilliantly marketed as a token of love and fidelity.

Do educated people smoke less than uneducated people?

The more education an individual receives, the less likely it is that they will be a smoker. **32.9%** of people who did not graduate from high school smoke, while **31.9%** of high school graduates smoke. Conversely, **26.8%** of people who received some college education smoke, but only **14%** of college graduates do the same.

How many prisoners are there worldwide?

There are over 9 million prisoners throughout the world. Most—**25%** percent or 2.2 million people—of these prisoners are in U.S. prisons. China is next with 1.5 million people behind bars, and Russia has 860,000 incarcerated inmates.

What percentage can you save by shopping at the supermarket by yourself?

Studies show that if you shop without your kids or spouse in tow, you'll save between **10%** and **40%**.

HOW MUCH CAN YOU SAVE BY CHOOSING TO MOVE AT A PARTICULAR TIME?

Try not to move from the middle of May to the end of September. These are peak times for movers as many college kids are moving in and out at the end of the semester in May and the beginning of the semester in September. Moving companies inflate their rates by about **10%** in order to make as much money as possible during this college transition time. In addition, you can expect to pay overtime charges if you move on a holiday or weekend. No matter what time of year it is, however, the best time to move is during the beginning or middle of the month. The end of the month is generally the worst time because that is when most rental agreements come to an end.

What percentage of gas caps on American cars are damaged, loose, or missing?

17% of gas caps! This is particularly meaningful now because it makes it easier for thieves to steal gas, which they do by siphoning it out of the gas tank or simply knocking a hole in the tank and letting it drain into containers. These faulty gas caps cost the American public up to $588 million every single year!

> If more than **10%** of the population likes a painting it should be burned, for it must be bad.
>
> George Bernard Shaw, Anglo-Irish playwright

What percentage of Americans thinks public authorities should distribute free condoms to teenagers?

55% believe that this should be public policy. **56%** of males feel this way, while **54%** of females do. Republicans, who tend to more conservative, would go along with the practice in **32%** of the cases, while Democrats were more than double that at **66%**. **49%** of married people believe in this practice, as do **64%** of those who are unmarried. Parents are supportive **57%** of the time, and **55%** of those without children support the policy.

WHAT EUROPEAN COUNTRY HAS THE HIGHEST DEATH RATE FROM HEART DISEASE?

The Republic of Ireland has the highest death rate from heart disease at **.00052%** (52 per 100,000 population), which is almost twice the European average of **.00027%** (27 per 100,000). The United Kingdom has the second highest rate of heart attack–related deaths at **.00042 %** (42 per 100,000 population). France has the lowest death rate at **.00013%** (13 per 100,000 population). The essential reason for Ireland's number-one status is a lack of awareness or responsibility about how diet impacts the body. Unfortunately, this starts early. In fact, **29%** of boys and **36%** of girls eat only one portion of fruit daily. Additionally, **39%** of Irish adults are overweight.

"Integrity is not a **90%** thing, not a **95%** thing; either you have it or you don't."

Peter Scotese

What percent of people are willing to volunteer their time for a good cause?

It's nice to know that **78%** of adults ages forty-four to sixty-two are willing to help others. As a reward, people who volunteer their time are healthier and happier than those who don't.

What percentage of doctors admit to being overweight?

Obesity is currently an American epidemic and our health care providers are in the same boat as the rest of us. **44%** of doctors actually admit to being overweight.

It depends on the survey one is looking at, but certainly one of the all-time favorites is Tom Hanks. In a recent poll, Tom Hanks garnered **52%** of the votes, almost double what the runner-up, Johnny Depp, got with **27%**. The other favorites were Will Smith with **9%**, and Julia Roberts and Tom Cruise each with **6%**.

HOW SUCCESSFUL ARE DRUG MANUFACTURERS WHO USE DIRECT TO CONSUMER MARKETING?

Direct to Consumer Marketing or DTC is a relatively new advertising ploy that drug manufacturers use to get you to buy the latest expensive prescription medicine—and also to convince a number of people that they have a serious condition that they need to deal with. Illegal in most of the world, these ads are designed to create an emotional, not a medical response. They also encourage patients to diagnose themselves and to not look at alternative treatments. As a direct result of these ads, roughly **33%** of patients asked their doctors about an advertised medication and, **44%** of the time, doctors gave that patient the drug they requested.

What percentage of children suffer from attention deficit hyperactivity disorder?

Attention deficit hyperactivity disorder or ADHD—a condition marked by lack of behavior control and a short attention span—is most frequently diagnosed in children in their preschool and early school years. It is estimated that between **3%** and **5%** of children—approximately 2 million children in the United States—have ADHD. This means that roughly one child in a classroom of thirty-five kids has the condition.

"If you treat people right they will treat you right—**90%** of the time.

Franklin D. Roosevelt, American president

How big was the media empire of William Randolph Hearst?

William Randolph Hearst, the real-life figure who inspired *Citizen Kane*, had a media empire that included twenty-eight newspapers—and his Sunday newspapers were responsible for nearly **20%** of total Sunday circulation. He also owned *Good Housekeeping* and *Cosmopolitan* magazines, a film studio, a wire service, and a feature syndicate.

What chance do new businesses have of survival?

It's a tough market out there. New businesses only have a **50%** chance of surviving past five years.

What percentage of households are headed by single parents?

9% of American households have only one parent at the tiller.

How many people in the United States are eighteen years or older and single? 92 million! This group comprises **42%** of all U.S. residents eighteen and older; **54%** of these are women.

How dangerous was it to be in the U.S. Air Corps during WWII?

Very dangerous! More dangerous, even, than it was to be a Marine. The men in the Air Corps had to complete thirty missions, and the chances of dying on one of those missions was **71%**.

"If you do it right **51%** of the time you will end up a hero." Alfred P. Sloan, U.S. auto executive

WHICH PRODUCT CARRIES A HIGH PERCENTAGE MARKUP?

The answer is jewelry. The average commercial jeweler will "keystone" his price, make the list price double what he pays—a **100%** markup! So if you buy a $2,000 ring, the jeweler will make $1,000 in profit if you pay the list price. You'll pay even more if you buy jewelry displayed in those beautiful four-color catalogs in a jewelry store. These prices are double keystoned. This means the prices are marked up by **400%** because the company who sells to the jeweler wants to leave enough markup room for any and all jewelers, no matter how greedy they may be. So if you're looking for a pair of earrings and their catalog price is $300, the price the jeweler paid for them was only $75. Even if they give you a substantial discount, they've still made more than a **100%** profit

Are parents concerned about their children's weight?

Despite rising numbers of obesity among children in today's sugar-filled society, **79%** of parents said they weren't concerned.

HOW IMPORTANT IS KEEPING CONTROL OF YOUR MONEY WHEN YOU HIRE A CONTRACTOR?

It is extremely important to not let your contractor get ahead of you when money is concerned. A small advance of up to $1,000 or **10%** of the total job cost can work out, but if you give a contractor **33%** of the money up front, then he is in control. If your contractor says he needs the money for supplies, you need to question why he is that close to the line, or why he doesn't have credit at suppliers. The only time you should pay for supplies is if they are custom made for you and nonreturnable.

WHO IS THE ONLY MAJOR LEAGUE LEFT-HANDED PITCHER TO HAVE A WINNING PERCENTAGE OF .900 OR ABOVE?

Randy Johnson went 18–2 in 1995 for a **90%** winning average. He is the only left-handed pitcher to accomplish this feat. Johnson won the American League Cy Young Award that year.

Are girls who play basketball more likely than boys to suffer a concussion?

Girls who play basketball are close to **30%** more likely than boys to end up with a concussion, and those who play soccer are **65%** more likely. The symptoms of a concussion are dizziness, nausea, amnesia, loss of balance, and confusion. There is also post-concussion syndrome that can make the sufferer lethargic for weeks.

WHAT ARE THE CONSEQUENCES OF KEEPING KILLER WHALES IN CAPTIVITY?

Killer whales have become popular attractions at various parks throughout the United States, but there is controversy about holding them in captivity. In the wild, many orcas live to be more than eighty years of age, but whales held in captivity can die in their twenties. Most don't make it past forty—forfeiting **50%** of their lives. The artificial environment at most aquariums is said to be the problem. Most killer whales, due to the relative smallness of the tanks they live in, do not get the life-giving exercise that they get in the wild. Also, when these animals are taken out of the wild, they give up living within family units where some would otherwise spend their entire lives. The loss of this family structure translates into psychological and then physical problems.

How many states have pollution problems?

Some **40%** of states in the United States have severe or extreme pollution problems. While this percentage is appalling, it's good to know that due to pressure from both the public and the government, most states are making a serious effort to clean up their mess!

How much pornography has entered the American movie scene?

Saying "a lot" would not do its intrusion justice. Today, Hollywood releases 11,000 adult movies a year, more than 20 times—**2000%**—its mainstream movie production.

What percentage of serial killers are female?

Out of all the American serial killers, women only make up **8%**. However, American females account for **76%** of all female serial killers worldwide. Aileen Wuornos is undoubtedly the most famous female serial killer. Depicted by Charlize Theron in *Monster*, Wuornos murdered seven men and was executed under the death penalty in 2002 in Starke, Florida.

> "Gravity is a contributing factor in nearly **73%** of all accidents involving falling objects."
>
> Dave Barry, U.S. comedian

What percentage of women suffer miscarriages?

Actually, the figure is quite high—**20%** of women have experienced a miscarriage at some point in their lives. This number may even be inaccurate. Many women will miscarry without even knowing it and just think the miscarriage is indicative of a heavy menstrual cycle. If these miscarriages are counted, the numbers may rise to indicate that closer to **40%** or **50%** of women have, in fact, miscarried.

WHAT PERCENTAGE OF AMERICANS HAVE AN ALCOHOLIC DRINK WITH BREAKFAST?

Bring on the Bloody Marys, mimosas, and Irish coffee! An average of **26%** of people like to have a drink with breakfast. **33%** of the imbibers are men, **19%** are female, and the majority of both groups range in age from eighteen to twenty-nine. When one turns sixty-five, the percentage of those drinking drops to **17%**. **17%** of those with a household income of less than $20,000 imbibe with breakfast compared with **33%** of those who earn more than $100,000 a year.

What percentage of people believe in the five-second rule?

53% of Americans trust in the five-second rule, picking up and eating anything from hot dogs to ice cream to toast. Studies show that this may be okay. The majority of foods can stay on the floor for up to thirty seconds without being contaminated by bacteria.

Are some people allergic to cell phones?

Surprisingly, it appears so. People seem to be getting contact dermatitis—a red rash on the cheek and ear—from the use of cell phones containing nickel. Unfortunately, roughly **50%** of phones do contain some type of nickel. I guess too much cell phone use, really is too much!

HOW MUCH MORE DO YOU SPEND AS A RESULT OF UPSELLING?

Upselling is where salespeople push you to buy a version of what you want that costs more money. For example, the Lowes' home improvement website lists over 700 refrigerators and, at the low end, there is just a modest price increase from one model to the next one up. With such a small increase in price salespeople will try to convince you to shell out just a few more dollars than you had planned for a model they claim to be much better.

While manufacturers claim to offer so many models to give consumers a choice, there is another hidden and more sinister motive. They know that if you come into a store planning to spend $500 on a refrigerator, chances are the trained sales staff can get you to spend between **15%** and **20%** more. So, prepare for battle before you decide to buy a large appliance— and stick to your guns!

"Interesting little article here. It says that, uh . . . the average human being only uses **17%** of his brain. Boy, you realize what that means? We don't use a full, uh . . . **64%**.**"**

John Ratzenberger as Cliff in *Cheers*

How strong is a leopard?

Pound for pound, a leopard is **700%** stronger than a human being. You don't want to get involved in a wrestling match with this spotted cat!

Who smokes more: men or women?

Many more men smoke than women. **55.2%** of men smoke compared with **22.4%** of women.

Have breast cancer rates dropped or risen in recent years?

Breast cancer rates have dropped more than **2.2%** per year for the past several years, due to early detection of suspicious or precancerous tumors and faster and better treatment. Breast cancer among African American women, however, has only dropped **1.6%**, and the rates have not changed at all for Asian or Native Americans.

What percentage of diagnostic tests given by hospitals are unnecessary?

No one has a definitive figure, but one study found that **40%** of tests ordered by hospital physicians were not needed. We live in a sue-happy society and doctors—who are afraid to miss anything lest they find themselves in court for malpractice—make sure they cover all their bases.

Why are women sentenced to prison terms?

70% of women who are incarcerated are sentenced for non-violent, drug, or property crimes such as forgery or credit card fraud. **90%** of these women are single mothers.

What percentage of unmarried people aged twenty-five and older have achieved a bachelor's degree or higher?

24% of all Americans over the age of twenty-five have earned at least a bachelor's degree. This percentage is sure to continue to rise as more and more importance is placed on education.

CAN YOUR COMPUTER KEYBOARD MAKE YOU SICK?

Think twice before tapping on those keys! Your computer keyboard can, in fact, make you very ill. **8.25%** are home to enough bacteria to be potential health hazards. Some keyboards even harbor **500%** more germs than a toilet seat! The main cause of this bacteria is the food crumbs that lodge in the spaces between the keys. Dust can also allow moisture and allow bacteria to develop and people with colds may cough on the keyboard.

To keep your keyboard clean, unplug the keyboard and shake the crumbs loose. Remove remaining debris with compressed air or wipe the spaces clean with a small paint or computer brush. You can also wipe grime off the keys with a rag dampened in water, dry it, and then follow that up with an alcohol wipe. Don't rub too hard or you can obliterate key markings.

WHAT PERCENTAGE OF SOLDIERS HAVE BEEN KILLED IN IRAQ?

Since the start of hostilities in Iraq, 4,222 troops have died in the Middle East. **98%** of them have been male, including **91%** who were not officers. **82%** have been active duty; **11%** have been National Guard. **74%** were Caucasian, and **11%** Latino. **19%** were killed in nonhostile causes. **54%** of U.S. casualties were under twenty-five years old and **72%** were from the Army. Of the U.S. troops, 30,920—**20%** of the total force there—were wounded with brain or spinal injuries.

If a guy is over **25%** jerk, he's in trouble. And Henry [Ford] was **95%**.

Lee Iacocca, U.S. auto business executive

WHAT PERCENTAGE OF MARRIED AMERICANS WOULD BE WILLING TO GO INTO COUPLE'S THERAPY TO TRY AND SAVE THEIR MARRIAGE?

82% of adults said they'd be willing to go to therapy, and this was affected to some degree by gender—among other factors. **81%** of men said they would be willing to go, but women topped that with **84%**. **83%** of adults with kids would be willing to give therapy a try. Overall, an overwhelming majority would be willing to try to work things out.

How common is financial infidelity, where people don't tell their spouse the truth about finances?

Almost **29%** of U.S. adults aged twenty to fifty-five have been dishonest with their partner about spending habits. Surprisingly, **72%** of people believe that trust is essential to a successful marriage or partnership. Women are more likely to lie about their spending (**33%** women vs. **26%** men).

What percentage of people are sports fans?

54% of the people love sports, **45%** do not, and the remaining **1%** have no opinion.

HOW MANY PEOPLE SUFFER FROM PANIC ATTACKS?

Panic attacks usually occur spontaneously and are a burden, both physically and emotionally. During an attack, paralyzing fear arises out of nowhere and the sufferer's heart starts to race. They may also feel breathless, dizzy, nauseous, and claustrophobic. These symptoms may last for a few moments or hours. People often have to see many doctors before the condition is diagnosed, and a combination of cognitive behavioral therapy and drugs are used to bring it under control. One out of every seventy-five people suffer from a panic attack, and only **25%** of the people who have the malady are treated for it. Women are **50%** more likely to experience panic attacks than men.

Which celebrity would make the best presidential candidate?

1. Oprah Winfrey—**30%**
2. Donald Trump—**28%**
3. George Clooney—**24%**
4. Martin Sheen—**12%**
5. Angelina Jolie—**6%**

WHAT PERCENTAGE OF CASHIERS MAKE SCANNING MISTAKES IN SUPERMARKETS?

There are ordinarily no prices on products anymore, so we have to accept, more or less on faith, that the checkout scanner is accurately ringing up the right price every time we shop at the supermarket. Unfortunately, this is not always the case. Shoppers are sometimes overcharged on more than **2%** percent of items due to supermarket scanning errors.

The term "scanning error" is actually a misnomer. The scanner scanned correctly, but the correct price was not entered into the database that provides information to the scanner. Eliminating most scanning errors is simple enough. Place your sales items at the back of your cart and put them last in line on the conveyor belt—and keep an eagle eye on them as they are scanned. If you do spot an error, many stores will give you the item free, give you a free coupon, or refund you for more than the pricing error. Overcharging a customer is very bad for the store's image and is even illegal in some states.

What percentage of inmates have AIDS?

The overall rate of confirmed AIDS in the prison population is **0.48%**. Close to **2.3%** of white inmates are living with the virus as compared to **3.5%** of African American inmates. This rate is nearly three and a half times the rate in the general U.S. population of **0.14%**.

How many Americans feel safe in their neighborhoods?

A whopping **93%** feel safe in their neighborhoods. In addition, **78%** said there wasn't a place within a mile of their homes where they would be afraid to walk alone at night.

"45% of Iraqi citizens think it is morally okay to attack American troops.**"**

Marty Meehan,
American attorney and politician

> "The trouble with quotes about death is that **99.999%** of them are made by people who are still alive." Joshua Bruns

What percentage of people will have TVs by 2050?

Experts predict a huge population increase by 2050 and naturally many of these people will be watching television. Today, there are 111.4 million televisions in use in the United States. That number is expected to increase to 163.7 million, or **47%**. This expansion will be led by minorities, particularly by Hispanics with households predicted to increase **136%** and African American families, which are predicted to increase **66%**.

WHAT PERCENTAGE CAN YOU SAVE ON ELECTRONICS AT ANY GIVEN TIME?

At different times of the year, you can expect markdowns to be as much as **75%**. The biggest sales event of February is President's Day when electronics, audiovisual equipment, and computers often go on sale. Many other businesses may offer President's Day sales on items such as furniture and mattresses. You can also often find a good deal on air conditioners, exercise equipment, and used cars during this time.

WHAT CHANCE DOES THE AVERAGE ACTOR OR ACTRESS HAVE OF MAKING IT BIG?

Not surprisingly, the percentage of all working actors and actresses who make it big is less than **1%**. There is evidence of this all around us. How many times do we see a new face in movies? Not often, especially when you consider that there are tens of thousands of actors available for parts. In fact, **72.1%** of all these actors and actresses make less than $5,000 a year at their chosen profession. Many are forced to supplement their incomes by waiting tables, dog walking, or taking a day job.

WHO SHOPLIFTS AND WHAT IS THE AVERAGE AGE?

Women shoplifters far outnumber men with only **5%** of shoplifters being male, and women making up that extra **95%**. It's assumed that more women shoplift because they feel comfortable in the retail environment and there is a low risk for violence or physical confrontation. The average age of apprehended shoplifters is thirty, but **89%** of children admit to knowing someone who has, at some point, successfully stolen something from a store.

What percentage of people living in the United States speak a foreign language at home?

Almost **19.7%** of the population aged five and up speaks a language other than English at home and this percentage is steadily going up. English is the only language spoken in only **80.3%** of households.

What baseball team has the best winning percentage?

The New York Yankees have the highest all time winning percentage of **56.7%**. The San Francisco Giants come in second with **54%**, the Los Angeles Dodgers with **52.4%**, the St. Louis Cardinals with **51.7%**, followed by the Boston Red Sox with **51.5%** and—a shocker—the Cubs with a winning percentage of **51.4%**. The lowest of the low— until recently—were the Tampa Bay Rays with only **40.1%**.

WHAT PERCENTAGE OF HIGH SCHOOLERS HAVE HAD INTERCOURSE?

Many more than you would think. **63%** of high school seniors have had sexual intercourse, and **40%** of high school girls have had sexual experiences that their parents are unaware of. The first sexual encounter of about **50%** of the boys and **80%** of the girls has happened with someone with whom they are in a steady relationship. **88%** of teenagers say that talking with their parents about sex makes them want to delay losing their virginity because parents can point out the pitfalls that they are not aware of. Despite this information, **33%** of all teenagers say their parents have never talked about sex with them.

> **66 90%** of my game is mental. It's my concentration that's gotten me this far. **99**

Chris Evert Lloyd, U.S. tennis player

What percent of men lose their dieting willpower when on vacation?

More than half! **56%** of men apparently go by the adage "What happens on vacation, stays on vacation."

How many parents allow their nine- to twelve-year-old children to watch R-rated movies?

Surprisingly, more than half of these parents would allow their child to watch movies like *The Exorcist*, *Pretty Woman*, and *The Passion of the Christ*! Only **45%** of children are not allowed. From the **55%** who are allowed to watch, **33%** of these always watched with a parent and **66%** sometimes watched with a parent.

WHAT ARE YOUR CHANCES OF LOWERING YOUR CREDIT CARD RATES?

If you have a good record with your credit card company, chances are you can slash your rates. Basically, all you have to do is tell them that you've received other offers with lower APR rates and are wondering if—in lieu of your leaving their company—they can cut your interest rate.

This sounds crazy, but there is a very good chance that the company will agree with your demands. **56%** of the time, credit card companies agree to drop rates from an average **16%** down to **10.47%**. Today, with consumers spending less, companies may be even more amenable to slashing rates.

HOW WELL DO COUPONS WORK IN SAVING MONEY?

It's a mixed shopping bag, one might say. Most of the time, only **1%** to **3%** of coupons are redeemed every year. This means that in any given year up to **97%** of people (some years **99%**) are not heavy coupon users. One reason for this reluctance to use coupons is that they have been getting more complicated recently; today, **25%** of coupons require two or more purchases and are more of a hassle to use.

What percentage of Americans own cats?

Around one in four people— **25%** of Americans—own at least one cat.

What percentage of people think having a gun in the house makes it a safer place to be?

47% of Americans believe that a home with a gun is a safer home. **43%** believe the opposite.

"All organizations are at least **50%** waste —waste people, waste effort, waste space, and waste time."

Robert Townsend, U.S. business executive

Are parents aware of what their kids are watching?

Thankfully, American parents are hands on when it comes to monitoring their kids' TV watching. **67%** of children have limits on what they can watch.

What percentage of people would prefer to orgasm every ten seconds to every ten years?

It would seem at first blush that the shorter interval would be desired, but not everyone sees it this way. **20%** of Americans opted for only orgasming once every ten years, while **80%** chose orgasming once every ten seconds—8,640 times in a twenty-four hour day!

19% of doctors say that they'd be able to give their patients a lethal injection. But they also went on to say that the patient would have to be really, really behind on payments.

Jay Leno, U.S. comedian

WHICH BASEBALL PLAYER CAME CLOSEST TO GETTING INTO THE HALL OF FAME WITHOUT ACTUALLY GETTING IN?

Jim Rice, the great outfielder and slugger for the Boston Red Sox, a man who used to make opposing pitchers quake in their boots, garnered only **72.2%** of the votes from sportswriters in 2008, being named on 392 ballots, just a couple of points away from the **75%** needed for election to the Hall.

But the next year, 2009, his last year or eligibility, he squeaked in with **76.4%** of the vote—412 votes—and was in. It was rumored that he would have gotten in earlier, but was disliked by various sportswriters because he would never speak ill of fellow players, the stuff of which good baseball stories are made.

WHY IS MY BASEMENT WET?

A number of things can cause a wet basement, but **95%** of the time the reason is simple—water is getting into the foundation and saturating it with water. Contrary to popular belief, masonry is not impermeable and if too much water drives against the foundation it will leak. Of course if there are cracks, it will get in even faster. **30%** of the time the water comes from clogged gutters that spill water onto the ground. However, it can also come from improperly routed downspouts or improperly sloped land around the house that washes the ground water against the foundation. Improperly aimed lawn sprinklers can also cause problems.

To solve these problems, either clear the gutters and reroute the downspouts or use fresh soil and pack it five to six inches high against the foundation sloping it back to nothingness over three feet.

WHAT PERCENTAGE OF YOUR GASOLINE BILL CAN YOU SAVE IF YOU USE THE CRUISE CONTROL FEATURE ON YOUR CAR?

When it comes to saving gas, using cruise control can be quite an asset. By making use of your cruise control, you can save an average of **14%** on your yearly gas bill. Every single time a driver hits the gas pedal, whether he or she is simply accelerating on the highway or switching from the brake to the gas at a red light, gas is wasted. Cruise control stabilizes the speed of the car, making this constant acceleration obsolete.

"I have no idea what White House statement was issued, but I stand by it **100%**."

Richard Darman, American economist

HOW MUCH MORE DO CARDED HARDWARE ITEMS COST COMPARED WITH THE SAME ITEMS SOLD LOOSE?

More than ever companies are packaging items in so-called carded form, which is simply a piece of cardboard with the product held in by some sort of clear plastic blister. In general, such items cost **25%** percent more than loose items, but that percentage can go even higher. Word to the wise: if you're buying items such as screws, bolts, etc. always check to see if they are available loose before making your purchase. You don't want to be paying for packaging!

"A toddler believes that if you love a person, you stay with that person 100% of the time."

Lawrence Balter,
child psychologist and
parenting expert

HOW MUCH OF A DISCOUNT CAN I GET AT A HOTEL?

A lot! Calling up a hotel directly will give you a much better deal than booking it online or calling the central office with the 800 number. After you get a rate, haggle. Hotel rooms are one area where you should always ask for a lower price. If the clerk you are bargaining with seems reluctant, talk to the manager. More than **70%** who haggled say they won a rate reduction or room upgrade. Discounts of **30%** to **40%** are not unusual, and the rates are often much better than what you could get with an AARP or AAA discount card. Also, once you have locked in a low price, you can try one more haggle. Ask for a free upgrade to a bigger room or a free breakfast or a free late checkout.

How many Americans speak Spanish at home?

Throughout America, roughly **12.3%** of all Americans—35 million people—speak Spanish at home. And **20%** of all residents in Arizona, California, New Mexico, and Texas speak Spanish at home.

Do insurance companies cheat homeowners?

Insurance companies often offer **30%** to **60%** less to settle a claim than the amount of money it would take to restore a home back to the condition it was before damage occurred. This tactic has worked so well that the property-casualty insurance industry (that covers homeowners and cars) has recorded record profits of 73 billion dollars up **50%** from two years before.

How long is the tail of the Andean mountain cat?

The Andean mountain cat—found in the high regions of Bolivia, Peru, and Chile—is slightly larger than a big domestic cat, can grow up to two feet long, and has a tail equal to some **70%** of its body length—a whopping eighteen inches! Talk about a tall tale!

"For me, writing is **75%** procrastinating and **25%** actually sitting down and working."

Zooey Deschanel, American actress

What percentage of U.S. soldiers have been women?

In the Persian Gulf War in 1990, **16%** of the soldiers were female. In World War II, **2.5%** were women. In the Vietnam War **3%** of all soldiers were women, and **2%** of U.S. soldiers in the Korean War were women.

> **"**Placing the ball in the right position for the next shot is **80%** of winning golf.**"**
>
> Ben Hogan, U.S. golfer

What percentage of women know their cholesterol count?

Only **32%** of women know what their cholesterol count is.

What percentage of grandparents are caregivers for their grandchildren? Roughly **30%** of grandparents have assumed responsibility for their grandchildren.

Is burning wood hazardous to our health?

Yes, it is. Wood burning causes **15%** of particulate emissions in the United States and can seriously affect our respiratory health—especially that of our children. Doesn't it make you look at outdoor grilling in a whole new light?

> **"**Choose your life's mate carefully. From this one decision will come **90%** of all your happiness or misery.**"**

H. Jackson Brown, Jr., American author

What percentage of North America is uninhabited by humans?

It may not seem this way sometimes—especially when you're sitting in gridlocked traffic for hours on end—but some **38%** of North America remains wilderness.

WHAT PERCENTAGE HAVE DOCTORS' SALARIES RISEN OVER THE LAST FEW YEARS?

Overall an average doctor's salary has increased an average of **3.3%** or $155,000 over the past few years, while expenses have jumped nearly **25%** over the same period. How does this break down? Well, if a doctor spends thirty minutes with each patient and charges $100 per half hour, the breakdown is as follows: $3.30 of the $100 goes for malpractice insurance, $3.59 for repairs, equipment, and maintenance, $6 goes to pay for various supplies from computer paper to tongue depressors, $7 to pay for utilities and rent, $11 to pay various office expenses, and $28 for salaries and benefits. This means that only $41.00 goes to the doctor.

WHAT SEEMINGLY EASY CALL CAN TURN OUT TO BE MOST DANGEROUS FOR A POLICE OFFICER?

80% of all cops would say a domestic disturbance call can go from zero to ninety in the blink of an eye. Police officers are always wary when going into this situation where people are fighting, in a state of inflamed emotions, where alcohol is often involved, and where people are just looking to vent on someone. One minute an alcoholic husband is raging at a wife, then his rage is transferred to the officer. This situation becomes even more dangerous if a weapon is close by.

Another situation that rates high on a danger list—with **20%** of all police officers calling it an incredibly dangerous situation—is what's known as a "traffic stop." If an officer pulls over a driver for a traffic violation and the driver or his passengers are felons, a seemingly simple procedure can becoming instantly dangerous. Remember, felons are usually armed!

“ 98% of the adults in this country are decent, hard-working, honest Americans. It's the other lousy **2%** that get all the publicity. But then—we elected them. **”**

Lily Tomlin, American comedian

> **"A good marriage is at least 80% good luck in finding the right person at the right time. The rest is trust."**

Nanette Newman, English actress and author

WHEN ARE GRIZZLY BEARS MOST DANGEROUS?

The last word in the grizzly bear's scientific name *Ursos arctos horribilis* indicates just how dangerous they can be. Grizzlies normally leave people alone—just don't get involved with a mama grizzly and her bear cubs. Run-ins with these overprotective moms account for **70%** of all deaths resulting from grizzly attack. Mama bear's main concern is protecting her young until they reach reproductive age—and she'll do whatever it takes to make sure her cubs get there.

If you do have the misfortune to find yourself facing down a grizzly bear, do not run—a grizzly can reach speeds of up to forty miles per hour over short distances. Instead, stand your ground and avoid eye contact, which grizzlies interpret as a challenging behavior. Pepper spray is also effective defending against them and special large cans are sold for use as bear repellant.

To avoid this situation altogether, it is best to make noise by talking, singing, or otherwise announcing your presence whenever trekking through a park where there are grizzlies. The last thing you want to do is surprise a grizzly bear—particularly one with cubs!

What is the normal attrition rate of soldiers during wartime?

Every year **18%** of soldiers leave the Armed Services, due to death, injury, or simply because they don't want to serve any longer.

What percentage of men will risk sunburn to watch a beautiful lady lie out in a bikini?

66% of all men would rather feel the burn than miss out on a chance to ogle a beautiful woman. Hope they brought some aloe vera!

90% of leadership is the ability to communicate something people want.

Dianne Feinstein, U.S. senator

"A democracy is nothing more than mob rule, where **51%** of the people may take away the rights of the other **49%**."

Thomas Jefferson,
U.S. president

What are the most popular last meal requests?

It depends on where the prison is located, but French fries are the most popular request. They are chosen by the condemned around **39%** of the time, beating any other selection handily. Of America's "dead men walking," only **7.5%** chose to eat breakfast as their last meal.

WHAT PERCENTAGE CAN BUYING STORE BRANDS HELP YOU SAVE?

Store brands are brands that are made for a particular store and are exclusively carried in that store. Just about every kind of store will have its own store brands including hardware stores, drug stores, office supply stores, electronics stores, supermarkets, etc. You can save considerable amounts of money—**20%** or more—by buying store brand products. When you buy name brands, you're basically paying extra for the name of the product and the familiar packaging.

Are people who have Parkinson's disease misdiagnosed?

Of the estimated 1 million people in North America who have been told they have Parkinson's disease, as many as **20%** have been misdiagnosed. Parkinson's is a progressive disorder marked by tremors and slow movement and doctors often misdiagnose the condition because they lack the special expertise to recognize and treat it.

What percentage of doctors would give teenagers contraceptives without getting parental consent?

Sorry parents! **58%** of all doctors would prescribe birth control to your teenager—without your consent!

What effect does losing weight have on blood pressure?

If you have high blood pressure, losing weight can make your blood pressure decrease by as much as **50%**, and many people who have had to take medication to control their blood pressure are able to go off it completely. The bottom line is that when weight is reduced, the heart—which is essentially a pump—doesn't have to work as hard to distribute the blood.

Do people believe more in the paranormal or God?

This may be surprising to some, but **58%** of individuals believe in the supernatural while only **54%** believe in God.

Abstaining from sex before marriage is a strong belief supported by **63%** of Americans. But **85%** of born-again Christians, **85%** of those who consider themselves to be "very religious," and **91%** of Evangelical Christians believe this is the way to go.

DO STORES SET UP MERCHANDISE TO MAKE YOU WANT TO BUY MORE?

All stores do this **100%** of the time. The supermarket is one kind of store where traps are placed for the unwary, and the ultimate goal is to separate you from your money. For example, milk is placed at the back of the store, so that you have to walk by all the other products in order to make that simple purchase. While you're walking, you see other products that you want to have and, before you know it, you've made an impulse buy! This is the same logic that causes you to have to walk the entire length of a drug store to get a prescription filled or why stores like Home Depot make you walk though the paint department to get to the wallpaper and blind departments. None of this happens by accident. It is carefully planned, intended to slow you down and get you to spend money you had no intention of parting with.

> **90%** of people's nightmares is standing in front of 1,000 people. Did you know that? And having to speak. You would have thought it would have been a madman tying you up and taking your eyes out.
>
> Robbie Coltrane, Scottish actor

What percentage of cats and dogs snore?

Many pets snore—and it sounds much louder if they're on your bed! In total, **7%** of cats and **21%** of dogs snore on a regular basis.

WHAT PERCENTAGE ARE YOU OVERCHARGED BY WITH ZONE PRICING?

This can vary. Zone pricing is little more than the practice of setting different prices for the same grade and type of gas, depending on where the station is located. For example, on the same day premium gas was selling for $4.89 a gallon in one Los Angeles neighborhood, it was also selling for $4.39 a gallon in another, nearby neighborhood. Zone pricing seems to be a formula based on traffic patterns, gas station location, and also the economic strata of the neighborhood. Overall, when buying gas, look for savings of **10%**, which doesn't look like much until you add up what you'll save in a year.

What percentage of Americans believe in haunted houses?

Almost half of all Americans— **41%**—believe that houses can be haunted, and **21%** also believe in the existence of witches.

HOW MUCH CAN YOU SAVE BY BUYING ITEMS ON SALE AFTER CHRISTMAS?

After New Year's, many Christmas items sell for **75%** off, including Christmas and holiday cards, decorations, and scented candles. Any candy with a Christmas or holiday type packaging can also be marked down as much as **75%**. Many stores also try to get rid of their Christmas inventory, so look for products that sell well as Christmas presents or as seasonal items such as kitchen gadgets, toys, cookware, bathrobes, and slippers.

HOW MUCH CAN I SAVE BY BUYING ENERGY EFFICIENT APPLIANCES?

This didn't seem like a major consideration if you were looking to buy a new appliance in the past, but today the energy use of a new appliance is perhaps the most important consideration when you are making the decision to purchase. Indeed, if you buy a high-energy model, you will spend more on the juice to run that appliance than you will to buy the product itself. By choosing an energy-efficient product like something with the Energy Star label, you will save up to **50%** in energy use.

"Competing in sports has taught me that if I'm not willing to give **120%**, somebody else will."

Ron Blomberg, U.S. baseball player

HOW MANY GIRAFFES SURVIVE TO ADULTHOOD?

It may seem counterintuitive, but giraffes have a better chance at reaching adulthood than lion cubs! Between **25%** and **50%** of baby giraffes are in it for the long haul, an amazing percentage considering the dangers they face.When first born, baby giraffes are protected by their mother who stays close by. Despite their ability to stand and run within six hours of their birth, most baby giraffes spend much of their early days lying down—hiding to avoid the bite of a sharp-eyed predator.The babies—who are about six feet long at birth—have their own natural protection as well; their spotted coloration is a natural camouflage against hyenas and other small predators who would seek to get to them.

Giraffes have only one enemy—the formidable lion—and, while giraffes appear defenseless, they are actually very dangerous prey. Giraffes weigh over 4,000 pounds, stand around nineteen feet high, and have a kick so strong that it can crack the head or spine or even decapitate a hapless lion. The giraffe also uses his height as a defense mechanism—he can see miles and miles and, if any predators are around, will be long gone by the time they arrive.

"About half my designs are controlled fantasy, **15%** are total madness and the rest are bread-and-butter designs."

Manolo Blahnik, Spanish fashion designer

> **80%** of our life is emotion, and only **20%** is intellect. I am much more interested in how you feel than how you think. I can change how you think, but how you feel is something deeper and stronger, and it's something that's inside you.

Frank Luntz, American corporate consultant and pollster

What percentage of interest do most pawnshops charge?

This is something to watch out for if you sell an item at a pawnshop that you plan to reclaim later on. The interest on the money they lend can be **24%** or higher.

What percentage of men refuse to let their fear of terrorism interfere with their vacation?

93% of men prefer to risk it!

WHAT PERCENTAGE OF THE TIME SHOULD YOU REJECT A DOOR-TO-DOOR OFFER OF HOME IMPROVEMENT?

You should reject this type of home improvement **100%** of the time! If someone knocks on your door saying that he has some extra material—roofing, hot mix asphalt, etc.—"left over from another job," you should do two things. One, say you're not interested and two, close the door. Door-to-door scams are quite common, and there are even groups—generally known as "The Travelers" or "The Williamsons"—who travel in new trucks, wear good uniforms, and look quite legitimate. But don't be fooled. If you give them a chance they'll not only rip you off on the repair job, but will steal something when you're not looking. These scam artists usually arrive in the middle of the day when only the woman of the house will be home and they can better intimidate her. Older people are also prime victims.

What percentage of people believe in miracles?

You may think that the majority of today's Americans are cynics, but that just isn't the case. A hopeful **79%** of Americans still believe in miracles!

"In reality, serendipity accounts for **1%** of the blessings we receive in life, work, and love. The other **99%** is due to our efforts."

Peter McWilliams,
American author

"His genius he was quite content in one brief sentence to define; Of inspiration 1%, of perspiration, 99."

Thomas Edison, U.S. inventor

What percentage of Americans impulse buy when at the bookstore?

Most book buyers head to a bookstore with a purpose, but **77%** of the time they buy something in addition to what they came for.

How much has the cost of white bread risen in recent years?

If you've been to the supermarket any time lately, you'll have noticed that prices are getting larger while the product is getting smaller. In fact, most foods and other staples have risen in price over the past few years. Even white bread, the most simple food of all, has increased in price by roughly **16.3%** in recent days.

WHAT PERCENTAGE OF BIRDS CAN'T FLY?

Less than **1%** of the avian world can't fly, but it's interesting to note—and probably not surprising—that out of the seventy-five birds that have gone extinct over the last 400 years **33%** of them were birds incapable of taking to the skies.

Most birds incapable of flight do not thrive on land. However, some—like the ostrich and the penguin in particular—have managed to find other ways to survive and thrive. There are actually seventeen different species of penguin that thrive in the ice-cold waters of the Antarctic where they do their own kind of flying—in the water. There are also some species of bird—like the flightless Kakapo parrot and the colorful gallinule—that survive only with the help of conservationists.

How many stolen cars are recovered?

While **90%** of stolen cars are eventually recovered, most will have suffered severe physical damage or have parts missing from them. Kind of makes you wish you put in that alarm system!

How many people have gained weight at their current jobs?

Thanks to all that bad-for-you food left in the work kitchen, **45%** of workers have packed on the pounds at their current jobs.

A few years ago so-called superfoods came into the marketplace. They are simply foods fortified with vitamins and supplements, such as omega 3. Over the past few years, these supplements have been in high demand and have been added to over 250 products—an increase of **90%** since 2005.

177

What percentage of Americans curse?

74% of Americans say they hear curse words frequently or occasionally in public. **66%** of people say that people curse more than they did twenty years ago, and **64%** admitted to occasionally using the F word.

There are certainly far more people cursing than twenty years ago, and Hollywood is mirroring this trend. In *Pulp Fiction* there were **269** uses of the F word, **265** uses of it in *Goodfellas,* **140** in *South Park: Bigger, Longer and Uncut,* **16** uses in the *The Breakfast Club,* and **10** uses in *Jerry Maguire.*

How many Americans have experienced hearing loss?

Around **11%** of the population has lost all or part of their hearing due to the increasingly loud noises that assault us everyday. One proof: people who live under less industrial conditions maintain good hearing into old age.

Sudden loud noise (like an explosion) tears tissue in the inner ear and damages hearing almost immediately. Sustained noise (like the sound of a jackhammer) flattens hair cells in the inner ear (cochlea) that convey sound to the nerves. Each hair cell is tuned to resonate to a different frequency. The wilting of the cells is felt as ear pressure, hissing, roaring, buzzing, or ringing. If the noise stops, hair cells rise back up.

How caring are American parents?

It seems that American parents are very caring, with **72%** of kids under six receiving praise from their parents at least three times a day.

What percentage of a movie is normally used to advertise it?

Roughly, **30%** of a movie's budget goes toward advertising the film. That's an awful lot of money if you consider how much it costs to make movies in today's world.

How many moms expect a gift from their significant other on Mother's Day?

Listen up husbands! **41%** of mothers would like jewelry, and **40%** would appreciate flowers. Only **12%** would be happy if they only received a card.

" We just did a survey that showed . . . something like **65%** of the [American] people couldn't vote for the First Amendment if it was up for a vote today.**"**

Peter Prichard

IS IT POSSIBLE TO CATCH OBESITY LIKE A COLD?

Turns out that people who have close friends who are overweight have more than a **171%** chance of becoming overweight themselves. The idea goes that we are influenced by our friends and, without being conscious of what we're doing, we fall into the same overeating trap. You don't even have to be close to your friends to "catch" obesity; even talking on the phone with obese friends can have an adverse influence on our weight. On the flip side, if we pal around with thin people we can also lose weight.

How many people run red lights?

Red light, green light! **50%** admit to running at least one red light in their lifetime. No one admits to doing this on purpose.

"I've got a theory that if you give **100%** all of the time, somehow things will work out in the end." Larry Bird, U.S. basketball player and coach

Has the amount of American smokers decreased?

In 1944, **41%** of Americans admitted to smoking cigarettes. Today, that number has decreased significantly with only **21%** of Americans being addicted to cigarettes. One reason for this decrease may be the fact that smoking's health risks—including cancer, heart disease, and many other conditions—have been widely reported.

How many nonhuman creatures populate the Earth?

A lot! For every single person on the planet there are more than 1 million species, which include 3,000 types of lice, 73,000 varieties of spiders, 6,000 reptile species, and around 200 million insects! There are also 4,600 species of mammals, which represent a mere **0.3%** of animals, and 9,000 species of birds which represent a mere **0.7%**.

> " The average American worker has fifty interruptions a day, of which **70%** have nothing to do with work. "

W. Edwards Deming, U.S. statistician

"I do actually believe in love. I can't say that I'm **100%** successful in that department, but I think it's one of the few worthwhile human experiences. It's cooler than anything I can think of right now."

Trent Reznor, U.S. musician

HOW MUCH MORE DO PEOPLE SPEND WHEN THEY USE A CREDIT CARD INSTEAD OF CASH?

Studies have shown that people spend more with a credit card—about **15%** to **20%** more. After all, it's only plastic and you don't have to come up with the actual cash for at least a month or maybe for years. So, if you really are trying to get a handle on your finances, leave those cards—and temptation—behind. Instead, take along a set amount of cash that you have to live with. This may feel un-American, but it will keep you from getting further in debt.

When do most traffic accidents involving senior citizens occur?

79% of traffic fatalities involving older drivers occur during the daytime, and **73%** occur on weekdays and involve another vehicle.

What percentage of three- to five-year-old kids prefer baby carrots to French fries?

In fact, **54%** of them liked the carrots when they were packed on top of a fast food French fries bag which was otherwise filled with fries. See, you really can trick kids into eating healthily. Unbelievable, but true!

"In Hollywood, an equitable divorce settlement means each party getting 50% of publicity."

Lauren Bacall, U.S. actress

What percentage of women who use condoms as their sole form of birth control will become pregnant?

Each year, only **2%** of women whose partners use condoms will become pregnant if they *always* use condoms correctly each and every time they have sex. Also, each year, **15%** of women whose partners use condoms will become pregnant if the condoms are not used correctly.

How many doctors have observed and not reported incompetent or impaired colleagues?

96% of doctors have observed a doctor who seemed to be incompetent or impaired in some way. Frighteningly, **46%** of doctors who have seen this occur haven't reported their fellow doctor for faulty medical practices.

> I don't know why people question the academic training of an athlete. **50%** of the doctors in this country graduated in the bottom half of their classes.

Al McGuire, college basketball coach

" Should such an ignorant people lead the world? How did it come to this in the first place? **82%** of us don't even have a passport! Just a handful can speak a language other than English. "

Michael Moore, U.S. filmmaker

How many people in the United States are older than sixty-five and unmarried?

15 million Americans older than sixty-five are unmarried. These older Americans make up **16%** of all single people eighteen and older.

What percentage of people know someone who has been unfaithful to his or her spouse? More than half of Americans —**54%**—know someone who has or has had an unfaithful spouse.

Why do teenagers smoke?

81% of all adults point a guilty finger at smoking in movies. The belief is that kids copy what they see, and smoking has often been made to create the tough personality of a character. **70%** of adults also think that any film showing actors smoking should be given an "R" rating.

"Actors should be overheard, not listened to, and the audience is **50%** of the performance."

Shirley Booth, U.S. actress

"Of all the peoples whom I have studied, from city dwellers to cliff dwellers, I always find that at least **50%** would prefer to have at least one jungle between themselves and their mothers-in-law."

Margaret Mead,
U.S. cultural anthropologist

What percentage of movies rented in hotel rooms are adult films?

Between **45%** and **55%** of the movies rented in hotel rooms are adult films. The average time a porn movie is watched in a hotel room is twelve minutes.

"The mother may do 90% of the disciplining, but the father still must have a full-time acceptance of all the children. He never must say, "Get these kids out of here; I'm trying to watch TV." If he ever does start saying this, he is liable to see one of his kids on the six o'clock news."

Bill Cosby, U.S. comedian

What is the chance that Lake Mead will run dry?

Lake Mead—the chief water source of Nevada—is one of the most significant sources of water. It was created during the construction of the Hoover Dam, and is part of that reservoir system. But a combination of unusually dry years, global warming, and explosive population growth has caused it to be estimated to have a **50%** chance of running dry by 2021.

How many arsonists are convicted?

Arson is far and away the leading cause of property loss, costing homeowners over $2 billion a year. Unfortunately, a large majority of these fiery perps get away with it. **16%** of all arsonists are never even arrested and only **2%** are ever tried and convicted.

> **"50%** of people won't vote, and **50%** don't read newspapers. I hope it's the same **50%.**" Gore Vidal, American author and playwright

What percent of people approve of birth control?

Surprisingly, birth control use is supported by **93%** of all adults. This includes **90%** of all Catholics and **88%** of all born-again Christians, those who consider themselves "very religious," and Evangelicals.

WHAT PERCENTAGE CAN YOU SAVE IF YOU CUT DRUGS IN HALF?

One of the very best ways to save a lot of money on drugs is to buy a double dose drug and then cut the pill in half. While this works with many pills, it does not work with all and can end up being a dangerous decision if you take the wrong dose. Before you take this route, be sure to talk to your doctor or pharmacist. You can buy small knife blade devices, called "pill splitters," that will quickly and accurately slice a tablet and slash your costs at the same time. The savings are often quite dramatic and can typically add up to as much as **40%**. Today, to save money, **23%** of people taking prescriptions cut their pills in half, so it has become a common practice.

CAN YOU SAVE A LOT BUYING PRIVATE LABEL PRODUCTS?

You can absolutely save money by taking this step! Many national brand manufacturers such as Heinz, Falstaff Beer, and Wonder Bread produce a lot of foods under private labels for supermarkets. Actually, **40%** of national brand manufacturers produce identical products under private labels for supermarkets. There is a big price difference—**25%** in fact—between national brands and private brands. With this type of savings, a family that usually spends $432.00 a month on groceries can save up to $1,872.00 per year!

WHAT PERCENTAGE OF AMERICANS WOULD HIRE A PRIVATE INVESTIGATOR TO FOLLOW THEIR PARTNER IF THEY SUSPECTED HE OR SHE WAS CHEATING?

It appears that the majority of significant others would prefer not to be kept in the dark. Only **16%** of Americans would call in a private investigator to tail their mate and **14%** of males would pick up the phone compared to **19%** of females. Of these, **16%** of married women and **17%** of unmarried women want assurances of fidelity.

Do hate groups still exist in America? Unfortunately, they do. In fact, the number of hate groups rose **48%** since 2000!

HOW MUCH HAS THE PERCENTAGE OF PEOPLE RECEIVING COLONOSCOPIES RISEN IN RECENT YEARS?

In 2000, Katie Couric took a bold approach to encourage men and women to be screened for colorectal cancer. She had a colonoscopy done on live television. The former co-host of NBC's *Today* show wanted to raise awareness about colorectal cancer after her husband's death at age forty-two from the disease. Her efforts have paid off. After the broadcast, the rate of colon cancer testing rose by **20%** throughout the United States. Researchers came to call this the "Katie Couric effect."

What percentage will buying health insurance with a high deductible save?

A high deductible will cut your costs dramatically, while at the same time provide coverage for catastrophic problems—the kinds that are life threatening or could send your family into bankruptcy. For a deductible of $7,500 you could save as much as **40%** over insurance with a lower deductible.

WHAT PERCENTAGE OF HOME CONTRACTORS GO OUT OF BUSINESS?

Unfortunately, between **80%** and **90%** of all contractors go out of business after five years. This competitive job market is why it is important to find out everything you can about a contractor, including whether he or she is licensed, before you hire them. If a contractor is licensed, the consumer affairs department of the Federal Trade Commission, in **100%** of cases, will help you proceed in a legal matter against said contractor.

When people think the main dish in a restaurant is healthy, they add an average of **131%** more in calories in side dishes, drinks, and desserts.

> " We talked about and that has always been a puzzle to me why American men think success is everything when they know that **80%** of them are not going to succeed more than to just keep going and why if they are not why do they not keep on being interested in the things that interested them when they were college men and why American men different from English men do not get more interesting as they get older. "

Gertrude Stein, U.S. author

"Too-broad questions such as, 'What's on your mind?' are apt to be answered 'nothing' nearly **100%** of the time."

Marge Kennedy, U.S. writer

Do more Christians or non-Christians believe in the paranormal?

More Christians believe in the paranormal. Non-Christians believe **66%** of the time, while Christians believe **75%** of the time. It appears that the idea of believing in the unseen isn't limited solely to God.

What percentage of the time do you have to replace the roof deck?

A whole new roof deck—the wooden base used to support the roofing—is needed only one in 1,000 times, that's below **1%**! A small portion of the deck may need to be replaced due to sustained water damage, but this does not happen often either.

> We find it easy to set limits when the issue is safety. . . . But **99%** of the time there isn't imminent danger; most of life takes place on more ambiguous ground, and children are experts at detecting ambivalence.

Cathy Rindner Tempelsman, U.S. journalist

WHERE DOES EARTH'S WATER COME FROM?

It's hard to say exactly where water comes from because it's constantly on the move! First it rises and evaporates, then rains back down on the earth, and utlimately flows back into the bodies of water. Around **98%** of this water comes from the ocean and is not drinkable. The other **2%** of water, which is fresh, comes from a variety of sources. **1.6%** of this H_2O is encapsulated in glaciers and polar ice caps, **0.36%** is found in underground aquifers and wells, and only about **0.036%** is found in rivers and lakes, but this still constitutes trillions of gallons.

"Hitting is **50%** above the shoulders."

Ted Williams, U.S. baseball player

What percentage of Americans have wished they were taller?

This percentage—**38%** of all Americans—is the same for both men and women.

How many prisoners have a high school degree?

Altogether, an estimated **57%** of all inmates have a high school diploma or its equivalent. However, **58%** of incarcerated women did not graduate from high school.

How can a heart attack survivor avoid a second attack?

Entering a cardiac rehab program can teach survivors what they need to know to avoid suffering another heart attack. Participating in this type of a program can cut the risk of a repeat attack by up to **30%**.

" I've learned it's always better to have a small percentage of a big success, than a **100%** of nothing. "

Art Linkletter, U.S. radio and TV talk show host

What percentage of brides buy their bridal gown wholesale from the manufacturer to save money?

Close to **90%** cut their wedding costs by purchasing their gowns in this manner. Many brides go into a bridal boutique, find the dress they want, receive their measurements, then say they need some time to think about their purchase. Instead, they bring those measurements to the manufacturer who can give them the dress of their dreams for close to **50%** off.

Who is America's favorite performer of the last twenty-five years?

Perhaps surprisingly, Mariah Carey came in first with **27%** of the votes. Madonna came in at a close second with **25%** of the vote, followed by Whitney Houston with **19%,** Bono with **18%**, and Michael Jackson with **11%**.

"The mind is the limit. As long as the mind can envision the fact that you can do something, you can do it, as long as you really believe **100%**."

Arnold Schwarzenegger, Austrian actor and California governor

What percentage of unmarried people aged twenty-five and older are high school graduates?

24% of unmarried people who are more than twenty-five years old fit into this category.

What percentage of airline fares go toward fuel costs?

Fuel used to account for **15%** of the costs of a flight's ticket price, but now it accounts for up to **40%**, which reflects a **150%** rise in fuel costs. Airline fares are rising along with fuel costs and will continue to change depending on the progress—or lack of recovery—of the U.S. economy.

Why is your roof leaking?

Most people are told that their roofs are leaking due to the failure of asphalt shingles or other roofing materials. However, most of the time this is a scam perpetrated by your contractor who is then happy to replace your entire roof for an average price of $5,000. In fact, **99%** of all roof leaks occur because the sealing around vent pipes or around the chimney has failed. Replacing the sealer—which is simple and cheap—easily solves the problem.

Are Americans still reading?

30% of readers say that they had spent less time reading books over the past year. **23%** of readers spent more time reading, and **53%** said that of the books they bought last year, between and one and five of them have yet to be read.

" We are decent **99%** of the time, when we could easily be vile. " R. W. Riis

"One-tenth of the folks run the world. One-tenth watch them run it, and the other **80%** don't know what the hell's going on."

Jake Simmons

"Success tends to go not to the person who is error-free, because he also tends to be risk-averse. Rather it goes to the person who recognizes that life is pretty much a percentage business."

Donald Rumsfeld,
American businessman and former Secretary of Defense

How many people favor taking patients off life support when there is no hope?

68% of the public agree with withdrawing life support or a feeding tube for those in a vegetative state or whose hope of recovery is almost nonexistent.

What percentage of men would trade a week's pay for a week's vacation?

70% of men prefer to lounge on the beach rather than head into the office. Paycheck be damned!

Can taking a nap during the day improve your job performance?

The answer here is yes! Even just a twenty-six-minute nap can increase your energy and job performance by up to **34%**. Studies have also shown that taking a nap during the day between the hours of 1:00 and 4:00 P.M. will reduce your "sleep debt" and enhance job performance.

HOW MANY PEOPLE ARE HAPPY IN THEIR MARRIAGE?

In a society where more than **50%** of marriages end in divorce, this percentage is a pleasant surprise. **88%** of the married people feel that they are happy or reasonably happy in their marriages. What's more, **71%** of couples said they've stayed married because of deep love while **73%** cited companionship. Of the two groups, men were more satisfied in their relationship, with **70%** saying that they would never think of leaving their wives. Women, while satisfied in their marriages weren't so optimistic. Over **50%** thought about leaving their husbands, despite the fact that they were still happy.

HOW MUCH GAS CAN YOU SAVE IF YOU DRIVE SLOWLY?

You can save a lot of gas if you keep to the speed limits. If you drive at sixty miles an hour you use **9%** less gas than if you cruise along at seventy miles an hour. And if you go fifty miles an hour you can save up to **15%**. Like most money-saving ideas this may take some willpower, but once you notice how much money you'll be saving each month, the practice will be well worth it.

> Guessing what the pitcher is going to throw is **80%** of being a successful hitter. The other **20%** is just execution.
>
> Hank Aaron, U.S. baseball player

How many Americans who suffer a heart attack have no symptoms?

40% or 64 million Americans report a lack of symptoms accompanying a heart attack. The problem isn't that those symptoms didn't exist, but rather a strong sense of denial. President Clinton, who had serious cardiovascular disease, said every time he exercised he experienced tightening in the chest that he subsequently ignored. He convinced himself his symptoms weren't serious when in fact his condition could have been fatal.

How many people who use dating services are already married?

5% of people who utilize dating websites or services are already married. Keep that in mind the next time you're scrolling through profiles on Match.com.

"I might not be smart enough to debate you point-for-point, but I have the feeling that about **60%** of what you say is crap."

David Letterman in a debate with Bill O'Reilly

What percentage of women know what they weighed in high school? **79%** of women have that number burned into their heads!

What percentage of Americans fly for business?

25% of all Americans fly as part of their workload and the added security at airports actually makes **40%** of travelers feel less safe than they felt before the strict guidelines were put into place.

" Once you're physically capable of winning a gold medal, the rest is **90%** mental. "

Patty Johnson, American track and field athlete and Olympian

> **"You have to give 100% in the first half of the game. If that isn't enough, in the second half, you have to give what is left."**

Yogi Berra, U.S. baseball player

What percentage of the population supports abortion rights?

Abortion rights are supported by **63%** of the American public.

Does drinking increase the risk of breast cancer?

Almost unbelievably! Having one drink a day increases the chances of breast cancer by **10%** and having three or more drinks a day raises a woman's odds of contracting the disease by **30%**.

> "Management by objectives works if you first think through your objectives. **90%** of the time you haven't."

Peter Drucker, U.S. writer

Why do so many people own dogs?

95% of dog owners have a pooch because they love the companionship and love that their dogs are capable of giving. **74%** of owners went so far as to indicate that their dogs are, to them, like another child in the family.

> "I have always found that if I move with **75%** or more of the facts that I usually never regret it. It's the guys who wait to have everything perfect that drive you crazy."

Lee Iacocca, U.S. auto business executive

> It is my indignant opinion that **90%** of the moving pictures exhibited in America as so vulgar, witless, and dull that it is preposterous to write about them in any publication not intended to be read while chewing gum.

Oliver Wolcott Gibbs, American editor, playwright, and theater critic

Do men who stop smoking later in their lives increase their odds of living?

Men who smoke shorten their lives by an astonishing 13.2 years. But if they stop smoking, even later in their lives, they reduce that risk by **50%**.

"I can't tell you **100%** what makes a relationship work. But I can see something good coming and I can see something bad coming."

Sandra Bernhard,
American actress and comedian

What percentage of Americans think a physically unattractive presidential candidate would have a difficult time getting elected?

The answer is certainly a commentary on the importance of visual media on our society! **70%** of Americans believe that an unattractive person would be at a disadvantage.

Investment Grade Wine or IGW—wine that will increase in value as it ages—comes from the place where most of the great wines come from: Bordeaux, France, an area with great weather and gravelly soil that is conducive to growing great wine. **25%** of the wines produced by Bordeaux are white and **75%** red.

"Words can never adequately convey the incredible impact of our attitudes toward life. The longer I live the more convinced I become that life is **10%** what happens to us and **90%** how we respond to it."

Charles Swindoll, U.S. theologian

How many doctors have received something free from drug companies? Conflict of interest anyone? **94%** of all doctors have received free handouts from drug companies that want their medications to be prescribed more often.

What percentage of credit reports contain inaccuracies?

Four out of five scores contain inaccuracies. That's **80%**! You can obtain a free credit report from the three main reporting agencies by going to *www.ftc.gov/freereports.* If you find inaccuracies, report them to the credit agency at once. If you don't recognize the account or inquiry, this could be a sign of identity fraud.

"My guess is that well over **80%** of the human race goes through life without having a single original thought."

H. L. Mencken,
U.S. editor and satirist

"It makes no difference whom you vote for— the two parties are really one party representing **4%** of the people."

Gore Vidal, American author

WHAT PERCENTAGE WILL YOU PAY ON YOUR CREDIT CARD IF YOU DON'T PAY ON TIME?

In the 1980s, interest rates on almost everything went through the roof because the prime rates, which are used by lenders as a base figure, were very high. Mortgage interest rates were high and people were tolerating that interest because it meant they could own a home. This was an eye opener to the credit industry and they started charging more and more because they saw that people would pay the extra interest. Today, if you don't pay on time you can be paying as high as **30%** interest or more.

What percentage of female models are thinner than the average American woman?

The average American woman is 5'4" tall and weighs 140 pounds. **98%** of all fashion models are taller—5'11"—and thinner, weighing an average of just 117 pounds.

> "If the new American father feels bewildered and even defeated, let him take comfort from the fact that whatever he does in any fathering situation has a **50%** chance of being right."
>
> Bill Cosby, U.S. comedian

> The Ninety-Ninety Rule of Project Schedules: The first **90%** of the task takes **10%** of the time, and the last **10%** takes the other **90%**.

Arthur Bloch, American author and satirist

How can eating oatmeal reduce the caloric content of one's diet?

Statistically, people who have oatmeal for breakfast are eating **30%** fewer calories. Oats are complex carbohydrates that are digested slowly and keep blood sugar steady, which reduces hunger and may help ward off Type 2 diabetes.

How many divorced people remarry?

The probability that divorced women will remarry has been declining since the 1950s, when women who divorced had a **65%** chance of getting remarried. Today, only **54%** of divorcees will remain single within five years of their divorce. **58%** of white women will remarry, compared with **44%** of Hispanic women, and **32%** of African American women. Unfortunately, many of these second marriages will also end in divorce or separation. **23%** will end after only five years and **39%** will end after just ten years.

What percentage of men suffers from erectile dysfunction?

One in five men—**20%**—aged twenty and up have ED. But that number could be reduced vastly with a variety of treatments, including taking drugs like Viagra or Cialis, or changing one's diet.

"In order to excel, you must be completely dedicated to your chosen sport. You must also be prepared to work hard and be willing to accept destructive criticism. Without **100%** dedication, you won't be able to do this."

Willie Mays, U.S. baseball player

> "You always have to give **100%**, because if you don't, someone, some-place, will give **100%** and will beat you when you meet."
>
> Ed Macauley, American basketball player

How helpful is penicillin?

Penicillin has been incredibly helpful and has saved many lives since it was developed in 1944. During World War II, penicillin is credited with bringing **12%** to **15%** of American soldiers back to the land of the living. However, as penicillin moves rapidly through the body, it requires frequent dosing. **80%** of a dose of penicillin actually leaves the body within three to four hours of consumption.

WHAT PERCENTAGE OF PRESCRIPTIN DRUGS CAN BE PURCHASED IN GENERIC FORM?

Most people think of generic products as being of lower quality than brand name drugs. Not true! Actually generics are drugs that are no longer protected by a company's patent; after the patent expires they can be sold at a much lower cost. This change does not affect the quality of the drug as the Federal Drug Administration oversees the safety and quality of all drugs in the United States. Basically, when you receive a generic drug, you're getting more bang for your buck. Today, close to **75%** of all drugs can be purchased in generic form.

Does it matter if industry sponsors medical studies?

It surely does. In fact, industry-sponsored research is positive **87%** of the time compared to **65%** of research that was not industry sponsored.

> At the constitutional level where we work, **90%** of any decision is emotional. The rational part of us supplies the reasons for supporting our predilections.

William O. Douglas, U.S. Supreme Court justice

HOW MANY COUPLES ARE TOLD THEY CAN'T CONCEIVE A CHILD, BUT ULTIMATELY DO?

Infertility—a growing problem among both men and women—affects more than 4.9 million couples in the United States. The reasons for this are varied, but include couples waiting until they are older to try to have children or a previous sexually transmitted infection. **86%** percent of couples who are told that they are infertile do, in fact, conceive a child within two years without assistance, but one in seven will continue to have difficulty.

How many drug addicts smoke?

Turns out that the more a person smokes, the more likely it is that they will also be addicted to drugs or alcohol. Among people twelve or older, **20.1%** do drugs, and out of this **20.1%** only **4.1%** of people are not smokers.

"I've been to all 50 states, and traveled this whole country, and **90%** of the people are good folks. The rest of them take after the other side of the family."

Jeff Foxworthy, U.S. comedian

> "Racing takes everything you've got—intellectually, emotionally, physically—and then you have to find about **10%** more and use that too."
>
> Janet Guthrie, American race car driver

What percentage of people fail at dieting?

Stop that yo-yo diet! Between **95%** and **98%** of people who lose weight gain it back within five years. In fact, only **2%** to **5%** of people keep their weight off. **90%** of those who gain their weight back gain more than they lost. Most people who successfully lose weight lose it by changing the way they live—not by participating in fad diets. Take that Atkins!

How much have home improvement complaints risen?

Home improvement complaints have been on the rise—up **60%** over the last five years—so it certainly pays to take some steps to protect yourself against contractors who simply don't know what they're doing, or have limited experiences. Making sure your contractor is licensed is one way you can protect yourself and make sure the job gets done to your satisfaction.

" If Americans knew how to deal with other people, they could bring peace to the world. Alas, they have not learned enough yet. The true American feels that he is **100%** welcome anywhere he goes. "

Nguyen Cao Ky, Vietnamese politician

> Sonny and another Hells Angel who was at the meeting thought they were beyond a little patch so they headed down to a local tattoo shop in Oakland and were the first to get the famous **1%** tattoos.

Chuck Zito, U.S. actor, boxer,
and former president of the New York chapter of the Hells Angels

How strong are ants?

Ants can carry ten times more than their body weight—that's **1000%**! The shortest ant life span is among workers who live an average of one to five years. Queens live the longest time—more than twenty years. In terms of size, ant colonies can be huge. For example, 306 million ants were discovered in a 2.7 square mile section on Ishikari Coast of Hokkaido, among which were 1,080,000 queens in 45,000 interconnected nests.

90% of video game AI really is pretty damn bad. I think that's actually why it's so much fun to shoot things. Because the AI is so bad and the characters are so annoying.

Matthew Perry, U.S. actor

How many people support public funding of HIV prevention and treatment programs?

These programs are supported by **87%** of the public, including **82%** of those who define themselves as religious.

> "The pitcher has got only a ball. I've got a bat. So the percentage in weapons is in my favor and I let the fellow with the ball do the fretting."
>
> Hank Aaron, U.S. baseball player

How often do married couples have sex?

The largest percentage—**31%**—are having sex less often than once a month. **27%** are having sex a few times a week. We're not sure why sex is not more frequent, but the husbands overwhelmingly said their wives weren't interested. Wives said they had lost interest in sex, were angry with their spouses, or both.

"Driving is about **75%** mental, so I believe in giving the ball some sweet talk on the tee. This isn't going to hurt a bit, I whisper under my breath. Sambo is just going to give you a little ride."

Sam Snead, U.S. golfer

Which of the following movie presidents would make the best president in real life?

1. Harrison Ford—**46%**
2. Martin Sheen—**20%**
3. Geena Davis—**17%**
4. Michael Douglas—**17%**

HOW MANY PEOPLE ARE KILLED BY PRESCRIPTION DRUGS?

270 people a day die from prescription drugs! That's **200%** more than the number of people who are killed in automobile accidents daily. The amazing thing is that most of these drugs are not misused, but are taken according to doctors' instructions. To put it plainly, ordinary prescription medications kill more Americans than either diabetes or Alzheimer's disease. If you watch drug commercials and listen carefully to the warnings about side effects—including death—it is easy to see that people taking drugs will be killed. But people today are also being prescribed more drugs than are necessary, and the conflicting side effects can be incredibly deadly!

❝ Just blow in it and sound bad for about a year and then make it sound a little bit better, and you get a little band together, and then you get a few jobs. You take four guys that sound half bad, but if they're **25%** each, they can give **100%**, you know? **❞**

Quincy Jones, U.S. musician

"Say you were standing with one foot in the oven and one foot in an ice bucket. According to the percentage people, you would be perfectly comfortable."

Bobby Bragan, U.S. baseball player

How much has heart disease been reduced since 1960?

The number of Americans suffering from heart disease has declined drastically—over **50%**—over the last fifty years thanks to better diet and the variety of public health campaigns started by the American Heart Association.

"I'm not sure if you can blame everything on the American way of life, but the United States are big. So, if you have a lot of people there, the percentage of stupid people is bound to be higher."

Stephen Malkmus,
American musician

WHAT PERCENTAGE OF AMERICANS DIE UNEXPECTEDLY EACH YEAR?

Of the roughly 2,400,420 people who die each year, around **40%** die suddenly. Heart disease is the number one killer, taking a life once every thirty-five seconds; every six minutes someone dies from an infection or medical error; every twelve minutes a traffic accident takes a life; every twenty-seven minutes someone is accidentally poisoned; once every twenty-nine minutes someone dies in a fall; every thirty-one minutes someone is killed at the hands of a drunk driver; every thirty-one minutes someone dies in a home accident; and every thirty-two minutes someone is murdered.

Do you believe that you are what you eat?

A whopping **75%** of consumers believe that nutrition plays the most important role in maintaining and improving health. **85%** also believe that it plays a key role in warding off specific diseases like cancer, heart disease, depression, and diabetes.

How common is dry skin?

Some 81 million Americans—around 40%—suffer from this skin irritation. To reduce dry skin, use moisturizing lotion like shea butter after bathing to hold the moisture in. Avoid hot showers and baths, drink at least seventy-two ounces of water a day to stay hydrated, and if your skin is itchy and worse on the inside of your elbows, see an allergist to find out if you are, indeed, suffering from eczema.

What percentage of married women who separate from their husbands ultimately get divorced?

91% of Caucasian women are likely to divorce their husbands after being separated for three years. **77 %** of Hispanic women ultimately ask for a divorce compared with **67%** of separated African American women. However, it is important to keep in mind that not all couples who separate actually go through the divorce process.

HOW EFFECTIVE IS THE USE OF BREASTFEEDING AS BIRTH CONTROL?

This practice is actually very effective. Only **2%** of women who use breastfeeding as birth control will become pregnant in the first six months after they give birth. The act of breastfeeding naturally changes a woman's hormones so that she does not become pregnant. Using breastfeeding as birth control can be effective for six months after delivery.

How much time do people spend in their cars driving and waiting for lights to change?

The average American with a seventy-five year lifespan drives for a total of four years and spends six months waiting for red lights to change to green. That's a total of **6%** of your life spent in the car!

Resources

American Pet Products Association
www.americanpetproducts.org

American Religious Identification Survey
By Barry A. Kosmin, Egon Mayer, and Ariela Keysar

Baseball's All-Time Best Hitters: How Statistics Can Level the Playing Field
By Michael J. Schell

Baseball Almanac
www.baseball-almanac.com

Bureau of Alcohol, Tobacco, Firearms and Explosives
www.atf.gov

CareerBuilder.com
www.careerbuilder.com

CBS News
www.cbsnews.com

Christian Film and Television Commission
2510-G Las Posas Road, Suite 502
Camarillo, CA 93010
(770) 825-0084

CNN.com
www.cnn.com

College of William and Mary
www.wm.edu

Council on Foreign Relations
www.foreignaffairs.org

Did You Know
www.didyouknow.org

Discover Magazine
http://discovermagazine.com

Farm Sanctuary
www.farmsanctuary.org

Federal Bureau of Investigation
www.fbi.gov

Federal Communications Commission
www.fcc.gov

Gallup
www.gallup.com

Global Issues
www.globalissues.org

Harris Interactive
www.harrisinteractive.com

International Union for Conservation of Nature
www.iucn.org

Johns Hopkins Bloomberg School of Public Health, Department of Health Policy and Management
www.jhsph.edu/dept/hpm

Life's Little Instruction Book
By H. Jackson Brown, Jr.

Mammal Species of the World: A Taxonomic and Geographical Reference, 3rd ed.
By Don E. Wilson and DeeAnn M. Reeder (editors)

Mayo Clinic
www.mayoclinic.com

Men's Health
www.menshealth.com

Metlife Mature Market Institute
www.metlife.com/mmi

National Bike Registry
www.nationalbikeregistry.com

National Geographic
www.nationalgeographic.com

National Highway Traffic Safety Administration
www.nhtsa.dot.gov

National Institute of Mental Health
www.nimh.nih.gov

National Institutes of Health
www.nih.gov

Newsweek
www.newsweek.com

Night Owl Network
www.nightowlnet.com

Parade Magazine
www.parade.com

Pew Forum on Religion and Public Life
http://pewforum.org

Planned Parenthood
www.plannedparenthood.org

Prevention Magazine
www.prevention.com

Reader's Digest
www.rd.com

Reuters
www.reuters.com

Seattle Children's Research Institute
http://research.seattlechildrens.org

SeniorJournal.com
http://seniorjournal.com

SNLKagan
www.snl.com/media_comm

Southern Poverty Law Center
www.splcenter.org

The Age of American Unreason
By Susan Jacoby

The Complete Wine Investor: Collecting Wines for Pleasure and Profit
By William Sokolin

The Education Digest
www.eddigest.com

The Gear Junkie
http://thegearjunkie.com

The Henry H. Kaiser Family Foundation
www.kff.org

The Motion Picture Association of America
www.mpaa.org

The New York Times
www.nytimes.com

T. Rowe Price
http://individual.troweprice.com

Two Minutes to Glory: The Official History of the Kentucky Derby
By Pamela K. Brodowsky and Tom Philbin

U.S. Census Bureau
www.census.gov

U.S. Department of Justice
www.usdoj.gov

USDA National Agricultural Statistics Service
www.nass.usda.gov

Woman's Day
www.womansday.com

Index

A

Aaron, Hank, 206, 229
Abortion, 65, 210
Actors, 123, 145, 188
Acute lymphoblastic leukemia, 63
Adams, Franklin P., 121
Africa, areas unihabited by humans, 71
African Americans, city with highest percentage, 107
AIDS/HIV, 141, 228
Air Corps, in World War II, 127
Airline fares, fuel costs and, 201
Airports, 85, 109
Air traffic controllers, experience of, 14
Air travel, 73, 209
Alcohol use, 40, 59, 83, 110, 132, 210
Allen, Woody, 5
Alley, Kirstie, 163
Andean mountain cat, tail length of, 155
Annapuma, 31
Ants, strength of, 227
Arctic Circle, oil under, 30
Arson and arsonists, 26, 191
Attention Deficit Hyperactivity Disorder (ADHD), 124

B

Bacall, Lauren, 185
Bachelor's degrees, 37, 137
Balter, Lawrence, 153
Barry, Dave, 132
Baseball, 54, 75, 100, 103, 129, 146, 151, 198, 206, 210, 229
Basement, water in, 151
Basketball, 23, 46, 129

Batting averages, highest, 75
Beach accessories, 67
Bed, preparing for, 101
Bedrooms, dirty, 44
Bees, disappearance of, 24
Berlin, Irving, 45
Bernhard, Sandra, 213
Berra, Yogi, 54, 210
Bible, literal interpretation of, 26
Bicycle theft, 47
Bird, Larry, 182
Birds, 102, 176
Bird strikes, 96
Birth rates, 20th century, 77
Blahnik, Manolo, 170
Bloch, Arthur, 219
Blomberg, Ron, 169
Blood pressure, weight loss and, 164
Books, 21, 27, 31, 50, 107, 113
Bookstores, impulse purchases at, 175
Booth, Shirley, 188
Bragan, Bobby, 232
Brain, using, 134
Breakfast, 32, 132
Breast augmentation, 106
Breast cancer, 210, 237
Breastfeeding, as birth control, 236
Bridal gowns, wholesale, 200
Brown, H. Jackson, Jr., 158
Bruns, Joshua, 144
Brunson, Doyle, 67
Building exterior, preparation of, 16
Burglar alarms, effectiveness of, 56
Burglary, odds of solving, 10
Buscemi, Steve, 66

C

Cable company rate increases, 97
Calories, 99, 195, 219
Cameras, surveillance, 48
Cancer, 32. *See also* Breast cancer
Car insurance, 108
Cars, 38, 40, 44, 52, 176, 185. *See also* Gas
    (fuel)
Carver, George Washington, 97
Cashiers, scanning mistakes by, 141
Cats, 89, 149, 167
Celebrities, 7, 23, 105, 140
Cell phones, 41, 53, 133
Cheating spouses, 30, 114, 188, 193
Children, 32, 42, 47, 63, 66, 87, 97, 98, 102,
    185, 197. *See also* Parents
Chinese children, overweight, 102
Cholesterol count, knowledge of, 156
Christians, belief in paranormal, 197
Christmas, sales following, 169
Cobb, Ty, 100
Coffee, health benefits of, 68
Coleman, Langston, 117
Colonoscopy, 194
Coltrane, Robbie, 166
Computer keyboards, illness caused by, 138
Condoms, 121, 186
Contraception, 164, 192, 236
Contractors, 129, 194
Cosby, Bill, 190, 218
Coupons, saving with, 148
Creationism, belief in, 12
Credit cards, 74, 148, 184, 218
Credit reports, 102, 215
Crime, 2, 42
Cruise control, 152
Cucumbers, water content of, 34
Cursing, 4, 178
Customer defection, 81

D

Darman, Richard, 152
Dating services, used by married people, 207
Death, 17, 104, 144, 231, 234
Death penalty, 25, 27
Dementia, curable, 104
Deming, W. Edwards, 183
Democracy, 162
Deschanel, Zooey, 155
Diabetes, diagnosed, 85
Diagnostic tests, unnecessary, 136
Diamonds, control of sales, 118
Diet and food, 14, 25, 60, 63, 76, 113, 147,
    177, 185, 219, 225, 234. *See also* Calories
Divorce, 7, 55, 56, 185, 220, 237
Doctors, 46, 81, 123, 145, 150, 158, 164, 186,
    215
Dogs, 43, 89, 117, 167, 211
Douglas, William O., 223
Downloads, riskiest, 49
Driver's education, 39
Drucker, Peter, 211
Drug addicts, smoking in, 223
Drug manufacturers/companies, 124, 215
Drugs (medicinal), 192, 222, 231
Dry skin, prevalence of, 235

E

Earth, 33, 183, 198
Earthquakes, areas prone to, 18
E-book readers, 21, 107
Edison, Thomas, 24, 174
Eggs, diets helped by, 14
Einstein, Albert, 82
Electrical devices, energy used by nonoperating,
    116
Electronics, saving on, 144
E-mail, 45, 62
Emotion *vs.* intellect, 171, 223

About the Author

Tom Philbin has been a longtime freelance writer. He has written a variety of books, both fiction and nonfiction. His latest are *The Killer Book of Serial Killers* and *Cheaper Insiders' Tips for Saving on Everything*. He is the only author ever to twice win the Quill and Badge Excellence in Writing award from the International Union of Police Associations for his 1997 book *Cop Speak: The Lingo of Law Enforcement and Crime* and the 2007 *A Warmer Shade of Blue*, coauthored with ex-NYPD officer Scott Baker.